WINDOWS ON THE HOLY LAND

J. C. PEDLOW

JAMES CLARKE

ISBN 0 227 67839 7

Published by
James Clarke & Co.
7 All Saints' Passage
Cambridge CB2 3LS
England

Goldcrest Press,
Trowbridge,
Wiltshire.

CONTENTS

THE HOLY LAND

1 Bethlehem
2 Hebron
3 Bethany
4 Jericho
5 Place of our Lord's Baptism
6 Qumran
7 Ein Geddi
8 Masada
9 Beersheba
10 Emmaus
11 Ramleh
12 Ramah
13 Bethel
14 Shilo
15 Nablus
16 Sebaste
17 Dothan
18 Affuleh
19 Nain and Endor
20 Cana
21 Tiberias
22 Magdala
23 Tabga
24 Capernaum
25 Ein Gev
26 Gergesa
27 Bethsaida
28 Safed
29 Acre
30 Megiddo
31 Athlit
32 Caesarea
33 Ashkelon

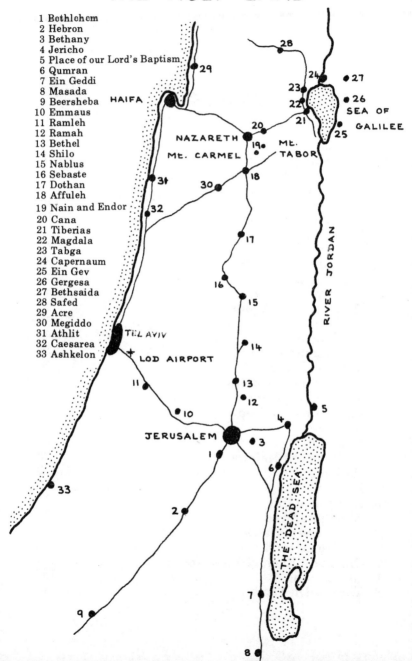

FOREWORD

This book is offered to the reader for several reasons. It originated on a winter's night when a cold wind was blowing the rain against the window panes and the trees in the drive were groaning under the pressure of the storm. To escape from the wintry feeling, I took H.V. Morton's book *In the Steps of the Master* from the shelf and said to my wife as I climbed the stairs on the way to bed, 'I'm off on an imaginary journey to the Holy Land, with the help of this book, since I'm sure I shall never go there myself'.

Was it by chance or Providence that a fortnight later after a meal at the house of some good friends our host asked a question for which we were wholly unprepared? 'My wife and I are thinking of going to Israel in May and we would like it very much if you and Nell [my wife] would join us as our guests.' So surprised were we that our reactions were slow. 'Don't you want to come', asked our host. I replied, 'Indeed, we should be delighted', and explained how I had been reading about the Holy Land. Their invitation was truly a strange coincidence.

Evidently they had been planning ahead, as they produced the brochure they had obtained from Orientours, the travel agency in Regent St, London. As we sat around the fire we discussed the lengths of the various tours, eventually deciding on a fifteen-day one. In mapping out our itinerary, a sense of excitement was already growing.

Our visit to the Holy Land turned out to be the holiday of a lifetime. It was a venture and an opportunity that we would not have missed for anything. Indeed, we appreciated the privilege so much that we took copious notes during the tour, and from these *Windows on the Holy Land* emerged. There must be many who have thought as we did but for whom the opportunity of visiting Israel has never arisen. You may be one of them; this book is placed in your hands to help you share such a pilgrimage in a holiday spirit.

A second reason springs from my own experience. While in Israel, I would have liked a book like this through which I could easily thumb. Although leaflets and maps are supplied by the travel agency, they are inevitably sketchy. To supplement them, this book may be read before the visit as a preparation, during the visit for consultation, and from time to time after the visit to relive an outstanding experience. It is hoped that *Windows on the Holy Land* will enhance the good work done by guides and brochures. It may keep us more alert to what is being said, and help in understanding what we see. It is hoped that the 'windows' may be useful both to those who have never been and to those who have been to the Holy Land — a holiday never to be forgotten.

A third reason for the book is to help visitors see the Holy Land as it is in reality rather than through any fanciful flight of the imagination or preconceived notions. In that way one is protected from any disillusionment.

Finally it has hoped that in progressing beyond the holiday spirit into the spirit of pilgrimage, the experience will be enriched. To pause at Bethlehem, to absorb the tranquillity of Galilee, to feel the drama of Jerusalem, to rejoice in the power of the Resurrection and the comfort of the Holy Spirit is the most satisfying experience the world has to offer.

One final consideration. I have described our journey out to Israel without mentioning the advantages the direct flights offered by El-Al to Tel Aviv. El-Al involves fewer complications.

I am indebted to my wife Nell, who, in spite of organising manse life and attending to responsibilities in the congregation and in the social life of the community, took time to read the script of this book. She has offered many useful and constructive criticisms which I warmly appreciate. Her flair for art has been of great assistance, and the pen sketches are her work. The opportunity of sharing a publication of this nature has been once again an enriching experience and we have found much pleasure in the common interest.

To all who in different ways have made this publication possible, I am deeply indebted. High on the list must come James Clarke & Co of Cambridge, who have shown much consideration and courtesy as well as making helpful suggestions. The cover design is their inspiration. I also appreciate the willing help of the Israel government Tourist Office.

To the encouraging readers of my earlier books who have kept prodding me to produce another book, I am glad to have managed at last to meet their request, and I hope that the book justifies their interest.

I would like to acknowledge the help that I have received from Orientours, and to congratulate them on the splendid arrangements that they have made in Israel, with regard to transport, accomodation, provision of guides and general information.

Last but most, I would like to thank the two gracious friends who, in their kindness, gave us such a wonderful holiday. They wish to remain anonymous, but I dedicate this book to them as a big 'Thank you'.

1. SHALOM

Many have a dream that sometime it may be possible to visit the Holy Land and walk in the places where Jesus lived and worked, to wander through Bethlehem where He was born, to stand in the Shepherds' Fields, to drink from Jacob's well where the Master talked with the woman of Samaria, to visit Capernaum and gaze on the soft, blue waters of the Lake of Galilee, to look at Jerusalem from the Mount of Olives, and to meditate in the Garden of Gethsemane. It must mean something to walk up the steps where Jesus was led captive and brought before Pilate, and to breathe the atmosphere of the old city of Jerusalem which our Lord loved and which rejected and crucified Him.

Since this dream has become a reality for me I feel that perhaps I could share with others my impression of the Holy Land. Where better to start than at the beginning?

We were a party of thirty-five members who set out under the leadership of two ministers, the Rev Harold Graham and a colleague, the Rev A. S. Cromie. These men were responsible for our welfare during the tour, shepherding us all the way to Israel and home again. Travelling from Belfast via Heathrow and Zurich we crossed the snow-clad Alps, left the Italian mainland behind as we looked down on Brindisi, picked out the Greek archipelago and the Island of Rhodes, and eventually we flew in to Tel Aviv, landing at Lod Airport.

Among the things that intrigued us on the outward journey were the white cliffs of Dover together with their counterparts across the Channel on the north coast of France. These reminded us of the days when Britain and France were joined geographically and we were then indeed a physical part of Europe. The Alps, too, were impressive with their jutting peaks reaching towards the sky and providing the general atmosphere of a winter wonderland. The cantons of

Switzerland were neat and tidy, the lakes were blue and as we moved further south and east, we anticipated a fortnight of unbroken daily sunshine.

We faced a touch of comedy and irritation when we were thoroughly 'frisked' at Zurich. Our baggage came under close scrutiny but in due time we were cleared. I was just on my way out of the Customs' booth when I was politely asked about a newspaper protruding from my pocket.

'What is the newspaper?' said the officer.

'The *Belfast Newsletter,*' I replied.

'Would you consider making a present of it to me?' my friend went on,'I would love to read about your trouble in Northern Ireland.'

When I handed it to him willingly, he accepted it with as much pleasure as an impecunious student would a five pound note.

It was late afternoon when we landed on the runway at Tel Aviv. As we alighted from the plane we could not avoid noticing a large hoarding rising from a terminal building, which displayed one word alone. It was the word Shalom (peace).

Many times during our stay in the Holy Land we were aware of this word Shalom. It is a word associated with our Lord who himself is called 'The Prince of Peace'. Since His mission to the world was a reconciling one, surely, if there is one place in our planet that could adorn the concept of Peace, it must be the Holy Land. Yet peace is hard to come by. During our visit the flower of peace appeared to be in full bloom but so unpredictable is the Middle East one has to be prepared for any event. We can only work and pray for the day when the cry from the heart of the prophet Micah may find response in all lands of the earth: 'They shall beat their swords into plowshares, and their spears into pruning hooks; nation shall not lift up sword against nation, neither shall they learn war any more; but they shall sit every man under his vine and under his fig tree; and none shall make them afraid.'

2. THE MELTING POT

While Israel looks for peace and talks peace she remains nonetheless on the alert. Her experience of being surrounded on all sides by hostile states who are slow to accept her existence has forced her to keep in readiness a highly trained army. At times an uneasy truce exists on the northern borders between Israel and Syria with sporadic skirmishing taking place between raiding parties on both sides. Centuries of suspicion, cut and thrust and sudden attack have left indelible marks in the minds and hearts of both sides which cannot be eradicated easily.

This is no new situation, for since the days of Abraham we can trace the searching of the Nomad race for a home and settled life in the small area which lies at the heart of three vast continents. Many examples of the tension between the Holy Land and her northern neighbours are found in the Old Testament. Almost at random my mind turns to an incident in the days of the prophet Elisha. Benhadad, the Syrian, besieged the town of Samaria and the inhabitants were in dire distress. Disease was rife within the city and the morale low. But, as often happens, at the darkest hour the dawn began to appear. Where little hope existed, psychological warfare came to Israel's aid. The Syrian army had gleaned rumours that the king of Israel had enlisted mercenaries from the Hittites and the Egyptians, and in consequence they kept hearing noises of chariots, and horses, noises of a great host advancing. So persistent were these rumours that the army fled in the night, leaving tents, horses, asses, meat and drink, silver, gold and raiment — the camp in its entirety.

Yet Israel needs peace to build up her land and establish her people in a true home after long drawn-out years of searching. For age old reasons the tensions persist and the Psalmist's words still express the concern 'I am for peace; but when I speak, they are for war.' No doubt the Syrians look at the picture from a different point of view, but fears and suspicions make reconciliation extremely difficult. On one occasion an

Arab asked us where we came from, and when we told him we
were from Ireland he looked at us with his piercing brown eyes,
made an understanding gesture and said: 'Much trouble in
Ireland!' One of our party was heard to comment 'You can say
that again!' At any rate we know by experience how difficult it
is to re-establish communication and mutual trust when
antipathy has been allowed to grow and to spread its roots deep
and wide. It will take effort, patience and a realisation of the
need to find some common ground and common sense. So we
appreciate the delicate poise and balance in the Middle East as
it stands at present. If we add the complication that over the
years the soul of Israel has been harrassed by forces from Asia,
Europe and North East Africa we begin to see the need for
understanding. This little strip of land on the eastern shore of
the Mediterranean Sea has been open to invasion through,
perhaps, no fault of its own but simply because of its
geographical position. In Old Testament times she suffered at
the hands of Syrians, Assyrians and Babylonians. Later her
territory was violated by Greeks, Romans, Egyptians, Turks
and Persians. Napoleon arrived in 1799 and in Jerusalem today
they do not fail to remind us that a British army entered the
city under General Allenby in 1917. So Israel indeed has her
war memorials.

When we visited the Golan Heights we were intrigued to find
instant memorials which have been established on the spot
where the actual battles of 1967 had been fought. Burnt out
tanks had been fenced in by the side of the road. The engraved
list of names is a reminder to all the young Israeli soldiers of
their comrades who had lost their lives during the Six Day War.
And talking of war memorials, we had the opportunity of
visiting the British War Memorial, a cemetery on the hillside
which looks across the Mount of Olives, down the slope of the
Garden of Gethsemane and along the Kedron Valley to the city
walls of Jerusalem itself. As I stood for a time with the
members of our party, scrutinising this burial place, my
thoughts turned to Rupert Brooke's soldier:

If I should die, think only this of me;

That there's some corner of a foreign field

That is for ever England.

Thinking of those whose earthly remains are buried at such
distance from their native land I sensed that in a way they may
not be so distant after all. Lying, as they do, outside the city

walls, they have something in common with the place that is called Calvary which also lies outside the city walls and where the Son of Man made the supreme sacrifice. In the issues of life and death the nearer we are to Him the nearer we are to home.

3. A POCKETFUL OF DREAMS

Dreams have always played a vital role in the life of the children of Israel. It could be said that they began with Abraham when he left Ur of the Chaldees and moved away from the Euphrates to go in search of a habitation for himself and his people. This dream sent them on the road moving north and west in the direction of the land of Canaan. Their life then was a nomadic one which they shared with the other nomadic tribes of the area.

Joseph in his generation had his dreams which at one point caused enmity between himself and his brothers, although in the long term they helped his household and his people. With reference to his brethren having sold him as a slave to Midianite merchantmen, he said 'Now therefore be not grieved, nor angry with yourselves, that ye sold me hither - God sent me before you to preserve a posterity in the earth - but as for you, ye thought evil against me; but God meant it unto good.' He was conscious that the changes which had taken place while the children of Israel sojourned in the land of Egypt were working out for their eventual welfare.

The next important stage came with the Exodus, when a Pharaoh who did not know Joseph regarded the Hebrews as foreigners and a risk to his country and his people. Moses emerged at this crucial moment, and, being by blood a member of the Hebrew race and by education schooled in the Egyptian court, he was well equipped to lead the children of Israel out of Egypt and to set them on the road again, seeking a land and a dwelling place of their own where they might live in peace. He had the ear of Pharaoh and the confidence of the leaders of Israel.

The dream of a homeland crystalised further as the Hebrew refugees began to take an interest in the land of Canaan once again, and this dream saw it as the land of promise. It was a land inhabited by a mixture of tribes and communities, each seeking a place in the sun. They were often engaged in conflict . In the melee the Israelites had the advantage of a certain cohesion which history had forced upon them. They appreciated that their ancestors had come this way and the belief became stronger that their home was to be here. Their monotheism gave them a unifying purpose in the face of the polytheistic communities. The divine promise given to Abraham 'Unto thy seed I will give this land' was taking root. The foundations of a nation were being laid. Toward the fulfilment of this dream the conquest of Canaan became imperative. Under the leadership of Joshua, Moses' successor, the initial steps were taken and the children of Israel crossed the Jordan. This turned out to be a long drawn-out and painful process.

At this stage the Israelites were harassed by the warlike Philistines, who, having been attracted to part of the fertile Mediterranean strip, decided on a scheme of conquest. They established themselves in cities like Ashkelon, Gaza and Ashdod. It was they who gave the name Philistia to the land they occupied and the name filtered through the country as a whole, living on as Palestine for three thousand years. As a consequence of the Philistine pressure the Israelites were galvanised into necessary defensive action. They organised themselves under a unified leadership, leaving behind them the period of the 'Judges' and entering that of the kings which was marked by the splendour of Saul, David and Solomon. This was a golden era in the eyes of the Israelites. Under David the kingdom reached its peak, and under Solomon the blessings of peace flourished. Through treaties and alliances, trade and commerce increased and the strategic position of the kingdom, straddling the caravan routes which ran in all directions from Egypt to the Euphrates, meant wealth and economic prosperity. Israel had access to the ports on the Red Sea and the Mediterranean. Jerusalem, as the capital city, became the power-house of the nation's spiritual energy.

Her troubles, however, were not over. She came under threat from great powers like Syria, Assyria and Babylon. When the Assyrians descended upon Samaria in 725 B.C., thousands of Israelites were deported to different places in that great empire and, if they felt like singing, there was no alternative but to sing the Lord's song in a strange land. This exile in Babylon, as it happened, was not a complete catastrophe, for in the next century Cyrus gave the Israelites permission to return and rebuild Jerusalem if they so desired.

Alas, conforming to the pattern, disaster overtook the

children of Israel and in subsequent centuries it was obvious that the previous dreams they held had been shattered. The prophets had played a leading role in strengthening morale and keeping the aspirations of the people alive but the glory departed. In 332 B.C. the Greeks over-ran Palestine and exercised a strong influence over the territory they occupied. They endeavoured to mould Jerusalem into the Greek style. This was successfully resisted by Mattathias, a Hasmonean priest, but the Hasmonean period proved to be the last of Jewish independence till the formation of the modern state of Israel.

From that time on, successive invading armies and powers beset Palestine and took what they could out of the land. With each invasion the pattern was much the same. Many Jews were scattered abroad to different parts of Europe, North Africa and Asia. They were the Jews of the Diaspora (dispersal). After Greek rule came Egyptian which in turn was followed by Roman. It was during the Roman occupation that Titus quelled a rebellion in A.D. 70 in which the Temple was destroyed. In A.D. 135 Hadrian put down a revolt by Bar Kochba, and Jerusalem (which had been destroyed) was rebuilt as Aelia Capitolina. By the Edict of Milan A.D. 313 Christianity was recognised in Palestine as a religion, due to the support of the converted Emperor Constantine.

The Romans occupied the country until A.D. 614 when they were superseded by the Persians. In the following period the influence of Mohammed established itself in Arabia, and the armies and missionaries of Islam conquered the Arab populations of Syria, Egypt, Persia and Northern Africa, and Palestine became dominated by Islam.

Then followed the period of the Crusaders, when the armies of Christendom made repeated efforts to win back the sacred places of the Christian faith. The Crusades came to an end with the fall of Acre in 1291. For the next two centuries the rule of the Moslem Mamelukes was firmly established. Damascus and Bagdad became the centres of an Arabian civilization that boasted an extensive and poetic literature, an enlightened philosophy and advanced agriculture and industry.

This peaceful and prosperous rule came to an end in the sixteenth century with the coming of the Turks. Palestine was governed under the Ottoman Turkish Empire until conquered by the British in 1917. During all these centuries of war and changing fortunes there seemed to be little hope of realising the dreams of the Jewish people. The Jews continued to make pilgrimages to the Holy Land, and there were some settlers who lived inconspicuously in places like Hebron and Jerusalem but they were not numerous or prosperous. Yet, dissatisfied as they were, their lot was proving happier than that of the Jews of the Diaspora who, faced by bitter hatred in the places where they had sought to establish a home, suffered severe and continual persecution.

It was only a matter of time till Jewry began to reach out again for some land in which to dwell, which it could call home, and in which it could live in peace. Its eyes turned again towards Palestine. In 1862, Moses Hess published his book *Rome and Jerusalem* suggesting the idea of a Jewish state, and later a Russian Jew, Leo Pinsker, proposed the same scheme as a practical one. His book inspired the movement 'Lovers of Zion' and the Jewish communities began to re-arrange their dreams. The slogan emerged, 'House of Jacob, come let us go!', known as BILU, the first Hebrew letters of the phrase. A young journalist Theodor Herzl, who was horrified at the treatment of the Jews in many countries, came to the conclusion that the only answer was the establishment of an independent Jewish state which would provide a refuge. His drive was so effective that it was possible to organise the first Zionist congress which was held in Basle in 1897 and which pointed the way ahead toward the ultimate dream of a Jewish nation in a Jewish state. Gradually, farming settlements came into being, and with the growth of modern technology and finance from abroad progress was registered.

The problem now was the natural sense of injustice felt by the Arab population. The Balfour Declaration issued by the British government in 1917 was an effort to approve of a national home for the Jewish people in Palestine without offending the Arabs. It was hoped that the twin aims of a Jewish homeland and an Arab state might prove feasible. It was also believed that great benefits would flow from mutual co-operation. Britain found herself holding the responsibility of administering Palestine under a mandate of the League of Nations. It is easy to see that the Arabs did not welcome the first tentative proposals to make room for Jewish immigrants. The position was aggravated by the rise and spread of Nazism and its horrifying efforts to exterminate the Jews in Europe. These unfortunate people could visualise Palestine as a welcome haven.

Increasing immigration led to riots. Britain pursued a policy of restricting immigration with no success, and as a result the problem was placed in the hands of an international commission. This body recommended partition into two states, Arab and Jewish, these to be autonomous. This was passed by the General Assembly on 29 November 1947. The Jews held territory which included the Negev Desert, part of the coastal plain, eastern Galilee and the fertile Jezreel Valley. The Arabs refused to accept this decision, and as the British withdrew war broke out. On 15 May 1948 the State, to be called Israel, was set up and began its existence. The territory was deemed to have been taken by force of arms. A homeland for the Hebrew people had been founded and modern Israel was regarded as a dream come true. Immigration increased, and the first three and a half years saw the arrival of an average of 500 immigrants every day. There are over three and a half million Jews now living in the state of Israel.

Subsequent wars have extended the boundaries of Israel at the expense of the Palestinian Arabs and the subsequent increase of tension calls for great diplomacy, discernment, understanding and goodwill. It would seem that some solution must be worked out which will enable these children of circumstances on both sides to find a way forward towards a just settlement of territory and a friendly and prosperous relationship. Although to the Western way of thinking this may seem to be an impossible dream yet the Middle East is unpredictable. At a time when it might seem unlikely, the dove of peace may descend on the Holy Land and not only Arab and Jew rejoice, but all men and women of all nations would respond with a joyful heart — AMEN!

When we visited the Wailing Wall in the city of Jerusalem, we realised that this is the focal point of many of the dreams held by the Jewish community. Situated at the south end of the west side of the Temple area, this impressive wall, 60 feet high by 150 feet long, attracts ardent orthodox Jews for lamentation, prayer and renewed devotion. Here are assembled the dreamers who mourn the loss of the temple and the glory that has departed. We were told by our guide that they have three headings for their prayers: the restoration of the temple, the establishment of their kingdom and the coming of the Messiah. Many types of Jews visit the Wailing Wall, each wearing the distinctive clothes of their original nationality and community. As well as the Sabras (Jews born in Israel), European and Asian Jews can be seen. Some are dressed in black clothes, wearing round hats and jet black side curls hanging down; some have an eastern look while others have a Spanish air. Their stance for prayer is fascinating. They stand feet apart with one placed a little forward and, reciting from an open book which they hold in both hands, they sway backwards and forwards rhythmically. In some instances genuine tears accompany the lament but others express their emotion with more inward concern and less outward demonstration. Written prayers on little scraps of paper are inserted into the crevices between the stones and some press their lips against the masonry as if imploring an answer from an unseen presence within.

One is always conscious that they are on the outside of a wall which now supports the Moslem mosque, the great Dome of the Rock, 'on the outside always looking in' as it were, and this humiliating situation must provoke some frustration. The lower courses of the wall are composed of ancient and enormous brown coloured blocks which are regarded as being part of Herod's Temple. The mosque — the Dome of the Rock — is an impressive structure which takes third place in splendour to the mosques of Mecca and Medina.

Among the practical dreams which inspire modern Israel are those associated with the development of the country. A promising programme of agricultural investment is seen in the inhabited hillsides and the open valleys. In our own land the valleys are studded with homesteads and the hills are left to the sheep. The Israelis have come to think that the good soil of the valleys is too precious to be devoted to dwellings, so they tend to build on the hillsides and to cultivate the valleys. This policy has proved successful for various reasons. From the point of view of protection it seemed sound strategy to inhabit the hills and so be in a better position to anticipate an invading army. In considering soil preservation and economics it was noticed that the rains of early spring and late autumn swept the fine soil from the hillsides down into the valleys below. The valleys became rich and the hills turned to wilderness. To counteract the denuding process, generations of farmers have terraced the uplands. Stone walls have been erected in curved formation round the slopes and the soil is thus contained. Olive trees have been planted in profusion and the vine has become part of the landscape. The long strips of rich corn and heavy wheat testify to the richness of the good earth.

A fine example is the fertile plain of Esdraelon, an irregular triangle stretching from the Jordan Valley to the Mediterranean, surrounded by the hills of Galilee to the north and those of Samaria to the south. In the heart of the plain is the old site of Jezreel (the seed plot of God):

The valleys stand so rich with corn

That even they are singing.

4. IT'S ALL UPHILL TO JERUSALEM

When on a holiday or pilgrimage to the Holy Land it helps if one keeps in mind a simple picture of its geographical layout as it was in Bible times. When our Lord journeyed from Nazareth to Jerusalem the country was divided into three main regions. To the north was Galilee; to the south Judaea and sandwiched in between was Samaria. The New Testament tells us that when Jesus was going up from Galilee to Jerusalem He 'must needs go through Samaria.' For the purpose of touring one may either begin at Jerusalem in Judaea in the south and proceed north through Samaria to Galilee, or alternatively start further north and go southward to the capital. In our case we began at Jerusalem in the south, which suited well because we were not far from Bethlehem where Jesus was born and where the Christian movement had its source.

Having boarded a bus at Lod airport in Tel Aviv about seven o'clock Greenwich mean time, we watched the sun set as we climbed into the Judaean hills on which Jerusalem stands. The pilgrims of the old days did not need to be told that it was an uphill journey to Zion since they had to walk or ride upon the mule or ass. Sustained by the Psalms, good companionship and the anticipation of spiritual revival and excitement at the journey's end, they found sufficient strength. They knew they were climbing all the way and the proof was in their weary limbs. We, too, knew we were climbing, not because of weary limbs or aching feet but by the simple deduction that the bus was working in low gear for most of the journey.

Soon the sun was speeding downward and daylight faded into a brief twilight. Within the hour darkness had descended, and when we arrived at our hotel on the northern side of Jerusalem the lights of the city were shining. It was too late to go sightseeing as the day was far spent, but we explored our Arab hotel and, weary pilgrims as we were after a long day of travelling, we decided to call it a day. It must have been around three o'clock in the morning when what seemed to be a blood-curdling yell wakened me out of my sleep, but when I became conscious and more alert I realised there was no need for alarm because it was only the voice of the muezzin calling the faithful to prayer. It did not take us long to become accustomed to the sound and it submerged into daily routine.

Next morning we could see where the sound had come from.

Not far from the bedroom window stood a graceful minaret with its circular gallery near the top, round which the muezzin was accustomed to walk when announcing the time of prayer. In this technical age the aid of the loudspeaker was proving most effective and was less strenuous on the vocal chords. From our window we could also see a long flight of steps leading down to a quadrangle of rock and flagstones and at one side there was an entrance to dark caverns. Intrigued to know what this evidently historic site could be, we investigated. At the foot of huge steps we found a series of caves. In front of the entrance to the largest was a runnel and a massive wheel-shaped stone which two or three strong men could roll along and seal off the passage-way into the caverns. This was a device we were to see on several occasions during our tour. An elderly man was on duty holding a lighted taper in one hand and a bunch of similar ones in the other. These he would light for the benefit of anyone who wished to explore the caves and see for themselves an ancient labyrinth of tombs which had once been used for the burial of the dead of a royal household. On either side of the main passages of the cave were several compartments containing stone slabs on which the remains of former generations were placed to rest. The name given to the cave is 'the tomb of the Kings,' but now it is believed to be the tomb of Queen Helena, mother of the Emperor Constantine. She was converted to Christianity herself and rendered devoted service to its cause. She exercised a strong influence on her famous son and was a valiant protectress of the Christian Church. She visited the Holy Land in the early fourth century and it is in keeping with her love for the faith that she wished to rest finally in a place like this. As we carried the lighted tapers through the passages, our fleeting shadows, mingling and intermingling on the walls, created the illusion of a great and mysterious company which in a misty form had materialised from the past.

The return to the hotel was a sudden transition from the ancient to the modern. It would not be long till lunch would be served so some of us took the opportunity of climbing a flight of stairs in the hotel which led to the flat roof. From this vantage point we enjoyed a panoramic view of the modern city. One feature sparked off our curiosity. We noticed that on many of the roofs of both large and small buildings were what appeared to be galvanised tanks perched quite out in the open. They were what they seemed. They were there to be exposed to the heat of the sun and were an essential part of a domestic hot-water supply. Nature is thus put into service and Israel has the appropriate climate to provide this modern amenity. At those times of the year when the sun is not so effective many households make use of electric heating as an added blessing to the system.

Near to the hotel was a garden of lawns, shrubs, rosebeds, bougainvillaea and poinsettia — a riot of colour! There was another riot — the sound of the Arab equivalent of pop music coming from a nearby cafe and adding a touch of gaiety to the atmosphere. We were poised to enter the old city of Jerusalem, the dream that stands waiting at the end of the uphill journey from Tel Aviv.

5. PEACE BE WITHIN THY WALLS

On a bright May morning it was exhilarating to walk along Salah-ed-Din, leading from the American sector of the modern city to the walls of the old city of Jerusalem. The old city is now but a tiny section of the fast-growing modern city which is spreading out in every direction. The sun was shining in a sapphire sky, and there was no need to think of rain before nightfall, or rain within weeks and even months. It was sunshine all the way. In keeping with this thought, our Arab guide called our party 'Sunshine', a word which he used as a rallying cry when he felt we were in danger of being separated among the crowds. There was always the temptation to wander into shops and get left behind. So at the call of 'Sunshine', we rallied the ranks with good humour and walked in the direction of the walls which were due to appear at any moment.

Rounding a final bend we passed the Central Post Office, and there in front of us, on the other side of a wide thoroughfare, stood Herod's Gate and the adjoining walls.

We had to pause before crossing the road which, takes its name after Sultan Suleiman, because of the heavy flow of traffic moving noisily in both directions. We were particularly aware of the cacophony of horn-blowing from vehicles ancient and modern. The motorists were horn-happy, sounding them as warnings, sometimes as signals to passers-by, and again, while parked on the roadside, to convey messages to friends making their purchases in a nearby shop. The buses were generously overcrowded , some passengers hanging on to the backs and overspilling the entrances in their anxiety to reach their destination. At the opportune moment we got through the busy traffic and finally stood on the other side where we could survey in peace, if not quietness, the walls which contain the old city of Jerusalem.

These tawny, crenellated stone walls, with their typical bastions, were built during the sixteenth century when Jerusalem had fallen into the hands of the Ottoman Turks. Their overlord, Suleiman the Magnificent, initiated many progressive building projects including the construction of a good defence around Jerusalem. The history of this ancient city was such that she was often the centre of conflict, and a coveted prize. As far back as 3000 B.C. her location attracted a settlement round her one natural water supply, and by 1400 B.C. she was quite a flourishing Canaanite community. Sited as she was on the hills, there was a natural defence, but to make sure, the inhabitants built a very thick wall in the Canaanite style.

These walls served their protective purposes for the citizens (then known as the Jebusites) until the days of King David, who arrived from Hebron around 1000 B.C. and made Jerusalem his capital city. Not only did he have his military headquarters here, but, by bringing in the Ark of the Covenant, he made it a spiritual centre, and since he ruled the united kingdoms of Judaea and Israel from Jerusalem, it also became the political centre.

In 586 B.C. Nebuchadnezzar captured Jerusalem, and carried into exile in Babylon many of its prominent citizens. Under Cyrus however, the Persian empire, which in turn engulfed Jerusalem, allowed some of the exiles to return, and Nehemiah gave the leadership necessary to repair the walls in 445 B.C. Many are the empires, including the Greek and Roman that had a hand in building, fortifying and restoring the walls. Herod the Great fortified two walls on the north end of the city with the three towers Hippicus, Phasaelis and Mariamne. Both walls were a little south of the present north wall. In the process of destroying and rebuilding there were some modifications in the line of the walls which helps to explain the possibility that the sites of the Church of the Holy Sepulchre and Calvary were in our Lord's time outside the city wall.

It is intriguing to think that the name Jerusalem means 'vision of peace' and that such stout walls were built against assault and to establish and keep peace within their confines. Yet in spite of every precaution they were attacked and smashed time and time again. The prayer of the Psalmist is an evergreen expression of longing and yearning, 'Peace be within thy walls.' The Moslems, the Crusaders and the Turks hammered at these walls. The British forces under General Allenby entered through their gates in 1917: Jerusalem — vision of peace! The walls stand as a demonstration of the conflict between what men hope for and what they have to do to keep their hopes alive. If

Stone walls do not a prison make
Nor iron bars a cage

neither can they guarantee freedom.

Among the many quarters recognised in Jerusalem — the Arab, Russian, Armenian, the Moslem, the Christian and so on

— there is a warm-hearted Jewish community. So far as one can see all the citizens are making a valiant effort to live in harmony and good will. We must wish them well. Strong in faith the Israelis of today appear willing to sort things out with their Arab neighbours. We look forward to the day when the Holy City may be Jerusalem by nature as well as by name, and that a genuine peace may reign within her walls.

The Israelis are also strong on security. Their soldiers, both men and women, were to be seen at the airport. Generally speaking, however, it was a discreet presence and we were never very much aware of them during the tour. The customs officials submitted our baggage to the most minute searching. Each article of luggage was taken out and carefully examined. Passports were scrutinised, and where an official was not quite sure of something a more experienced one was consulted. They were leaving nothing to chance. As we travelled throughout the land we sensed that they regarded their survival, as well as their well-being, as dependent on preparation and alertness.

With these reflections we stood poised to enter through Herod's Gate into the old city where Arab, Christian and Jew are living together. Through Abraham, Islam and Judaism share a common ancestry and through the Old Testament Judaism and Christianity share many common truths and thoughts. So three vast religious movements have their sacred places within this old city which draws pilgrims from all over the world.

6. THROUGH HEROD'S GATE

Having stood and admired the walls of Jerusalem shining in splendour under a burning sun in a cloudless sky, and having sensed the wealth of history they contained, we were now in the position to enter one of the three gates in the northern wall. Herod's Gate stood in front of us, on the other end of the wall to the far right was the New Gate, and in the centre the Damascus Gate. Herod's Gate protrudes a little from the facade of the wall itself and is equal in height. The open gateway with its rounded arch invites the beholder to enter the magic world that lies within.

The modern world of buses, motorcars, traffic lights and the rest of the the furniture of the twentieth-century is left behind for a city of narrow streets and a jostling world of pedestrians; Arabs riding on donkey or mule and young boys running madly in and out among the people pushing their carts and shouting at the top of their voices what sounded to us like 'Hello.' At first we thought this was some kind of eastern greeting, but we could see by the expression on the boys' faces that they were in deadly earnest to get on with their business. They were warning those in their path to get out of the way or else! We responded in our own naive way by shouting 'Hello' in return, but at the same time we hastily made way for the reckless messengers and so avoided what might have been an international incident!

It was quite exciting to find ourselves now walking in a busy, noisy, restless hive of buying and selling. The shops were like caves cluttered with merchandise of every description. There was the glitter of beads, pendants, trinkets and jewellery; camels, donkeys and mules exquisitely carved out of the native olive wood; fruit shops, fish shops, butchers' shops, drapery shops, clothes shops, shops with shoes and sandals lined up for sale — whatever line one would care to name, the goods were there, clustered into minute spaces on either side of the narrow streets. Many of the wares were on display outside the shop as a lure to the passer-by. The setting up of stalls in the open air was no problem, because there would be no interruption from rain. The shops themselves were something like an Aladdin's cave, and the vendors extended enthusiastic invitations to enter and survey for ourselves the goods on sale. When we did,

sometimes we were offered a glass of mint tea or a minute cup of
very strong Turkish coffee. Word was sent out to some nearby
cafe, and soon an urchin appeared bearing the refreshments on
a round brass tray which swung crazily on thin chains from a
hook which he held in his hand. This gesture of hospitality had
the effect of prolonging our stay in the shop and encouraged us
to buy more. The atmosphere was that of the oriental bazaar,
and the cacophony sustained our feelings of excitement.

To the right, just inside the gate was a flight of steps (called
David's Steps), which led to the top of the wall where there was
a narrow walk to the Damascus Gate. However, we took the
turn slightly to the left, and followed a narrow street which was
to lead us eventually to the Dome of the Rock. Inside the old city
are four main quarters, Christian, Jewish, Arab and Armenian.
We were now in the Arab quarter, following a labyrinthine way,
which ascended gradually on long shallow steps. From time to
time we looked up at buildings which stretched overhead from
one side of the street to the other and which explained why we
were walking alternately in sunshine and in shade. Some of
these buildings were homes and, no doubt, others afforded
means of overhead crossing in the old style.

On every side were little Arab children who recognised us as
tourists and pressed round, clamouring for 'baksheesh.' We
soon learned an Arabic word by necessity, 'Imshi' (go away).
Their pleas were hard to resist but if one yielded to these
demands the results would have been disastrous financially.
The experience brought to mind an incident in the New
Testament. When the children were brought to Jesus the
disciples tried to hold them back but our Lord said: 'Let the
children come to me; do not stop them; for the kingdom of God
belongs to such as these.' We can appreciate the disciples' point
of view at the time, but you have only to look into the eager
faces and searching brown eyes to understand the love the
Master felt for children.

Sometimes we wanted a photograph of them, so we waited till
we found two or three together and snapped them when they
least expected it. We gave them a tangible token of our
appreciation for their co-operation since cash was always
expected. We noticed that some of the mothers were not too
enthusiastic about our taking photographs but the younger
generation were quite eager and uninhibited. Our Arab guide
told us that some of the older people hold a superstition that a

PRAYING AT THE WAILING WALL

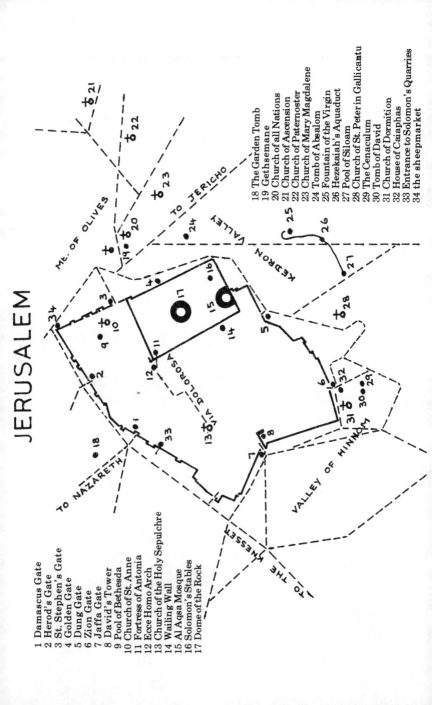

JERUSALEM

1 Damascus Gate
2 Herod's Gate
3 St. Stephen's Gate
4 Golden Gate
5 Dung Gate
6 Zion Gate
7 Jaffa Gate
8 David's Tower
9 Pool of Bethesda
10 Church of St. Anne
11 Fortress of Antonia
12 Ecce Homo Arch
13 Church of the Holy Sepulchre
14 Wailing Wall
15 Al Aqsa Mosque
16 Solomon's Stables
17 Dome of the Rock

18 The Garden Tomb
19 Gethsemane
20 Church of all Nations
21 Church of Ascension
22 Church of Paternoster
23 Church of Mary Magdalene
24 Tomb of Absalom
25 Fountain of the Virgin
26 Hezekaiah's Aquaduct
27 Pool of Siloam
28 Church of St. Peter in Gallicantu
29 The Cenaculum
30 Tomb of David
31 Church of Dormition
32 House of Caiaphas
33 Entrance to Solomon's Quarries
34 the sheepmarket

person who takes their photograph retains a certain power over them. Whether this is true or not, the children hold no such belief, especially if there is money in it for them. It was while taking a photograph of a little girl and boy that I made a serious mistake. There was no problem in lining them up and snapping the camera. It was in making the subsequent payment that the controversy arose. Dipping into my pocket, I discovered that I had no small change save an Israeli pound. In my innocence I considered the two children would feel like king and queen at receiving such a reward, so I handed the coin to the girl and signed that she was to share it with her friend. The little rascal had no intention of doing so and a fight was in progress in no time. She managed to slip out of the grasp of her raiding companion, and disappeared behind a wall out of sight with the little fellow in hot pursuit. I was glad to move off in the other direction before others were drawn into the fray! It can be a serious disadvantage and a cause of considerable embarrassment not to know the customs of a place!

As it was in the days of our Lord, beggars take up their stand at strategic places. Some are deformed and some suffer from blindness caused by infection. Others, drawing a discreet attention to their sores, speak in such a quiet, plaintive tone that it is difficult to pass them by. Yet one could not give to every crying need. As one looks at the beggars, the merchants, the jostling crowds, the laughing, talking, gesturing people; Arabs drinking their small cups of coffee, their voices raised in bargaining; women dressed in black in spite of the heat — there is one recurring thought — Jesus passed this way. He understood poverty where it was real, the deaf who could not hear, the blind who could not see, the crippled who could not walk, the merchant who would sell two sparrows for a farthing, the seething sea of humanity and the unresolved ends for which they lived. He had been this way and He understood. He brought to the crowds His warm heart of compassion and exercised His healing power. One could feel strongly the practical reality of the human life of our Lord, lived in this corner of the world.

As we proceeded on our way the background of eastern music began to fade. We approached another wall in which was built an arched doorway. Beyond a picturesque palm tree, we could see a golden dome reflecting the bright sun.

7. THE DOME OF THE ROCK

Once through the gateway, we found the contrast so sudden as to be almost breathtaking. Here, there was a wide open space paved in Roman style, with the impressive mosque called the Dome of the Rock, one of the greatest monuments of Islam, standing at some distance away on a commanding site, which inevitably draws the eye and inspires curiosity from any direction. This platform on which we stood looks out on the Kedron valley, the garden of Gethsemane and the Mount of Olives. Because of the steep descent into the Kedron valley beyond the walls, one seemed to be looking over a panorama of scenery from a mountain top, which is exactly the case, for the mosque is built on Mount Moriah whose crest, incidentally, juts through the floor of the mosque itself. It is the presence of this mountain peak which gives the mosque its name.

The golden dome was our first glimpse of the building for it can be seen for some distance, but now that we were in the vast open courtyard, the dome, while still outstanding, was seen to be only part of an architectural dream. The mosque is octagonal, built on a marble platform approached by flights of steps on every side. The building is a blending of Roman and Byzantine styles with a lavish display of Arab symbolism. The Dome of the Rock is what the name suggests — a circular cover built round the rock and supported by mosaic walls and marble pillars. On the outside there is a wealth of intertwined arabesque designs and generous quotation from the Koran, all worked in mosaic tiles. Before entering any of the four doors, it is necessary to remove footwear as a token of respect. One is reminded of the incident in the Old Testament when Moses stood before the burning bush in a desert place, and the Lord spoke to him saying: 'Put off thy shoes from thy feet, for the place whereon thou standest is holy ground.' Christians of the western world are not born into the tradition of taking off footwear before going into a place of worship, but in an eastern setting it comes more easily. Once inside one treads on thick Persian carpets in the ambulatory which surrounds the tip of Mount Moriah. This is the centre-piece of one's thoughts, since this rock speaks of Abraham, King David, Solomon and the temple that was built on the very site where the mosque now stands. We recall too, that our Lord stood hereabouts in the days of Herod's temple, so that visitors from varying backgrounds and faiths all find themselves standing on holy ground.

We looked at the concentric rows of marble pillars and the windows of semi-transparent coloured stone (not stained glass) which cast unusual tones of light. We admired the mosaics all around the walls with their intricate designs, and the splendid curve of the dome, its interior surface completely covered with tiny mosaic patterns in blue and gold. Taking into account the rose red carpet on which we stood we were absorbing from every direction an intriguing blend of reds, blues, amber, green and gold. The fifty-six windows provided the 'dim, religious light'. The atmosphere was a soothing contrast to the burning heat outside the mosque.

Protected by a wrought-iron screen stands the bare rock of the mountain, which appears to break through the marble floor, and gives the impression of emerging from another world, as indeed it does. The mosque is the expression of man's art and design, but this rock is a stark symbol of God's handiwork from the world of nature. It speaks of the enduring, the solid and the rugged, but it also speaks of the changing generations of mankind. Here Abraham wrestled with the primitive question of human sacrifice. This little piece of Mount Moriah was the scene of Abraham's struggle when prompted to offer up his son Isaac.

As we stood in the mosque we thought of the ancient link between the Arab and the Jew through Abraham. Abraham had two sons by Sarah and Hagar, Isaac being Sarah's child and Ishmael the son of Hagar. In time Hagar found a wife for her son in the land of Egypt, and the Arab world can trace its link with Abraham through Ishmael. The Jewish link with Abraham is strong through Isaac who was nurtured in Abraham's house. By this association in the ancestry, the two races can surely feel that the heart of God is warm towards both. Who can tell but that some day Abraham, 'the friend of God and the father of the faithful' may be part of a reconciling force between these ancient peoples?

In the mosque we also thought of David, who captured the city from the Jebusites and purchased this corner, once a threshing floor, thus acquiring a site second to none on which his son Solomon was to build the famous temple. David insisted upon paying fifty pieces of silver for the site and to him it was a sacred place, 'And David built there an altar unto the Lord,

and offered burnt offerings, and peace offerings. So the Lord
was entreated for the land and the plague was stayed from
Israel.'

We thought too of Solomon. David had it in his heart to build
a worthy temple, but, it was left to his son to fulfil the dream.
With the help of Hiram, the king of Tyre, who supplied
materials and provided many skilled craftsmen, the scheme,
which was undertaken in 966 B.C., took seven and a half years
to complete. The building was constructed with stones which
had been perfectly prepared before being brought to the site —
'so that there was neither hammer, nor axe, nor any other tool
of iron heard in the house, while it was in building.' The temple
was a rectangular building divided into various partitions
determining who could advance beyond each section. At the
very heart was the Holy of Holies exclusive to the High Priest.
Unfortunately Solomon's temple, on which the king exercised
so much thought, devotion and expense, was destined to
destruction, and the temple area was to undergo the successive
desolations and rebuilding which recurred throughout the
traumatic and dramatic course of Israel's history.

Solomon's work, which in its time was the pride and delight
of Israel, was burned down by Nebuchadnezzar in 586 B.C.
When it was restored fifty years later the result was somewhat
disappointing compared with the original. For one thing the
Ark of the Covenant had disappeared and no one knows to this
day what happened to it. At the present time excavation is
going on in an area west of the Wailing Wall, because of a
theory that it is a likely spot to recover such a treasure.

It was not until Herod the Great appeared on the scene that
an effort was made to erect another temple. It was an
opportunity he could not resist, for he had an obsession for
building. Nothing could be more popular than to build the
temple. With the help of a thousand priests trained as
carpenters and stonemasons, the work commenced in 20 B.C.
and was continued over a period of about fifty-four years,
during which Herod died and his son Herod Antipas carried on
the project. This was the temple which we read about in the
New Testament and which was often frequented by our Lord.
We think of the visits with all the little human touches as when
He commended the widow who, in putting a mite into the
offering, had given all that she had and so had given more than
many rich people who, in giving more, had made less sacrifice.

We think of the stir He caused when He upturned the money changer's benches because they were making the house of prayer a den of thieves. Especially do we think of the last week of His earthly ministry when He made the triumphal entry of Palm Sunday. We recall the Monday and the cleansing; the Tuesday and his discussions with the chief priests and the elders; the crowded hours of Wednesday, Thursday and Friday ending in the crucifiction. Jesus had said on one occasion by way of prophecy that the temple would be destroyed again and not one stone left on another. So it turned out to be. In A.D. 70, Titus attacked Jerusalem with typical Roman thoroughness. The city was devastated. Once again the temple was a natural target and was destroyed. The fate of Jerusalem through succeeding generations followed a similar pattern — occupation, repression and revolt. A final effort to achieve independence was organised sixty years later by Bar Kochba but was mercilessly crushed by the Emperor Hadrian. Nevertheless Rome was losing her grip. Although Jerusalem was rebuilt as Aelia Capitolina in Hadrian's time, and Christianity recognised as the official religion subsequently by Constantine, Rome was eventually forced to yield to Persian pressure. It was in the seventh century under Persian rule that the magnificent mosque which we know as the Dome of the Rock was built. Although damaged by an earthquake in the eleventh century, the restored mosque now takes an honourable third place behind Mecca and Medina.

We left the Dome of the Rock, and putting on our shoes, stood once again in the spacious temple area which extends over thirty four acres. Glancing to the right we could see Pilate's house at the far end of the square commanding an imposing position. From this vantage point Pilate could keep a close watch on the Jewish activities at the temple and his troops were on hand for any emergency. He was anxious to ensure that any revolt would be nipped in the bud.

In proceeding on our way we turned from the mosque with the golden dome to visit the mosque with the silver dome. It is called Al-Aqsa. Its name means 'The Further Place of Worship'. The latter is larger than the Dome of the Rock, rectangular in form and built in the Roman style with a porch extending the full length of the front facade. The symmetrical classical arrangement is emphasised by the seven arches

corresponding to the seven doors to the seven aisles. The
Byzantine columns, the magnificent pulpit, the intriguing
dome and the subdued light from the stained-glass windows
together with the arabesque designs create a profound
experience for the beholder. The spacious building is carpeted
in the Persian style, which produced a sense of silence and
peace, even as worshippers came in and out, paying their
respects to Allah. We noticed that part of the mosque was
partitioned off and repairs were proceeding; the result of an
explosion in the early 1970s.

8. BY THE GOLDEN GATE

Like the Dome of the Rock, the mosque of Al Aqsa stands on historic ground. One has only to descend by a flight of steps into the subterranean vaults for the shadowy ghosts of the Crusaders and King Solomon to come to mind. Here we are on the location of King Solomon's stables. In II Chronicles ix 25 we read that 'Solomon had standing for four thousand horses and chariots, and twelve thousand cavalry horses, and he stabled some in the chariot-towns and kept others at hand in Jerusalem.' When we let our imagination dwell on this account of the king's forces there must have been considerable stir and excitement in this vicinity at the southern end of the old city—the roar of the chariots, the clatter of the horses' hooves and the splendour of the king's soldiery.

Centuries later another colourful cavalry, that of the Crusaders, used the same stables which stood ready-made for them. The vaults are quiet now, but what memories of armies that must have passed this way since the days when Jerusalem was called Jebus, what scenes of war were enacted here! The confrontations of the ages lie buried in the silence of the soil and one is tempted to speculate on the meaning of it all.

Now it was time to retrace our steps over the expansive pavement in the direction of Pilate's house to which we have briefly referred. Whether this was the governor's actual home on the occasions he visited Jerusalem is controversial, but it is fairly certain he spent some time here. The Passover season was an anxious time, particularly for him, when he feared riots and disturbances. While extra troops were drafted in for the event, Pilate left his headquarters in Caesarea to exercise personal supervision at Jerusalem. This building (or its predecessor) was bound to have been garrisoned since from it everything taking place in the Temple and its environs could be easily observed. The presence of the Roman troops so near to the Passover festivities no doubt proved irksome to the Jewish community. There must have been an underlying suspicion too that the handing over of the High Priest's vestments (which were kept under security by the Romans in the strong room of the Castle of Antonia) was simply a cover for the Roman presence. It was from this vantage point that Titus and his soldiers witnessed the destruction of Herod's temple by a fire, maliciously started, which completely gutted the whole building from the court of the gentiles to the Holy of Holies. The extent of this devastation was not intended by higher authority in the empire, but the situation had got out of hand.

We moved over to the eastern boundary and looked at Mount Scopus through a succession of Corinthian arches. In the foreground are Jewish and Arab cemeteries on the slopes leading down steeply from the walls to the Kedron valley. As the ground rises on the other side of the valley, we recognised the Garden of Gethsemane. Beyond the garden the terrain slopes upwards more steeply to the Mount of Olives, which, at its highest, rises a little above the hills on which Jerusalem stands. If it is said that the view of Jerusalem from the Mount of Olives is quite something, the same is true in reverse. Gethsemane, together with the Mount of Olives and the little road to Bethany, which leads just over the hill, is inspiration to the eye and warmth to the heart. The panorama towards the east from Mount Moriah is also breathtaking. Down to the right, where the valley of the Kedron meets the valley of Hinnom, emerging from the south and west of the city, is a number of tombs which stand in their whiteness against the background of the olive trees. The tombs are said to be those of Zacharias, who, according to St Matthew, was slain between the temple and the altar; of Absalom, who wanted some memorial for himself because he had no son to keep his name in remembrance; and of St James, the brother of our Lord.

Moving to the left we see the Golden Gate, the origin of which is obscure. It is said to have received its name when the Emperor Heraclius passed through it in A.D.739 after his victory over the Persians. It is maintained that this gate stands on the site of the one through which our Lord entered in triumphal procession on Palm Sunday, and proclaimed His messiahship in dramatic form and in accordance with Scriptures. Originally this event was associated with the Shushan Gate, which would have been the natural way by which Jesus and His disciples would pass as they went to and fro between the temple and Bethany. It was the nearest way to Gethsemane and the Mount of Olives and it led them to the road that took them to the home of Martha, Mary and Lazarus.

The Golden Gate has a double entrance which has been walled up by the Arabs, who hold a traditional belief that as long as the gate remains blocked, Jerusalem will not be taken from them. The Arab guide told us of a legend that the Kedron valley would be the location for the events of the Day of Judgement. Jesus Christ would take His place on the top of the Mount of Olives, and Mahomet would stand in the arcade of the courtyard of the mosque. So each community has its folklore. We left the temple area for the time being, knowing that we were walking on the very pavement that Jesus had trodden nearly 2000 years ago.

9. STREAMS IN THE DESERT

One reason why old Jebus (modern Jerusalem) was chosen as a natural building site was its strategic setting in times of war. It could be fortified effectively and easily defended. It had a water supply adequate enough at the time, but as the city grew, the inhabitants of former days had to draw supplies from outside the city to augment the springs to be found inside. With modern knowledge and techniques the problem is not now so pressing. Our Israeli guide informed us that Israel possesses abundant supplies of water. Owing to the nature of the top layers of limestone soil the rains filter down into underground catchment areas. With modern engineering at their disposal they have only to tap these resources, and this they are doing. The supply and distribution of water enables modern Israel to make the desert blossom as the rose.

We read in the New Testament about one of the springs that was to be found within the city. It was named the Pool of Bethesda and was a popular resort in the days of our Lord. Its waters were reputed to have a therapeutic value and accordingly it was regarded as a local spa. Apart from mineral contents like iron, there was also a belief that at certain set times a stirring of the waters took place when the curative qualities were enhanced. So the Pool of Bethesda was a popular attraction, not only as a place where people gathered, but because it was a centre of healing as well. This aspect of the pool is reflected in its name. In the Hebrew language 'Beth' means 'the house of', and 'esda' signifies mercy or healing. This is truly a lovely way of assigning names by associating the function with the name. Jesus was born in Bethlehem, the House of Bread. Jacob's life was changed at Bethel, the House of God. Bethsaida is the House of Fishing and Bethany the House of Dates.

The Pool of Bethesda is situated not far from St Stephen's Gate, the only gate that is open on the eastern wall. It lies to the north east near to the Church of St Anne, a Crusader church which has been renovated as a mark of respect for Anne, the mother of Mary, Jesus' mother. It is said to be built over the

place where Mary was born. Originally this Pool of Bethesda
was composed of two main ponds contained in cisterns cut out
of solid rock. One accomodated the men and the other the
women. In St John's account there were five porches — one
porch running along each side and end with a fifth across the
partition. Today only one of these porches remains but it helps
us to visualise the more spacious original structure. There was
a third pool where sheep were cleansed before sacrifice in the
Temple. From the one remaining porch we can reconstruct in
our imagination the rows of Corinthian pillars which supported
the arched roof above the pool complex.

Down a narrow, steep, stone stairway is the pool, which
today is less imposing than it must have been in our Lord's
time. What can now be seen had to be unearthed from the
rubble of centuries. Sufficient has been excavated to enable us
to recapture in our mind's eye the scene as it was available to St
John — the multitude of sick folk, of blind, halt, withered,
waiting for the 'moving of the water'. Apparently at certain
times a spring bubbled up and caused a stirring or commotion
in the waters and the first person to enter the pool at that point
would be healed. 'For an angel went down at a certain season
into the pool' is how the evangelist puts it. The reputation for
healing was so strong and expectation so high that the faith of
those who believed was rewarded. Bethesda was indeed the
house of mercy and healing for the invalid who encountered our
Lord and was set free from an illness which had been with him
for thirty-eight years.

The necessity of water, so important in New Testament
times, as the Bethesda miracle shows, is no less so today, and
the Israelis point with pride to their agricultural achievements.
Streams in the desert — an attractive concept! Like ourselves
the people of the Holy Land depend on waters that come down
from the heights. They rejoice in the flow from Mount Hermon
of the River Jordan which makes a journey the length of the
land to the Dead Sea. But they also have a healthy respect for
the wells, ancient and modern, which spring up from below for
the benefit of man and beast. When we think of how David
longed for a drink from the well of Bethlehem we can appreciate
the blessings of pure, cool, clear water. When one visits a hot
climate after living in the temperate zones, one feels more
thankful for the quantity and quality of water we have at our
disposal in our lakes and reservoirs — and on tap at home. We

can drink freely and often. To have visited the land of the
prophets and absorbed some of its environment is to sense more
deeply Isaiah's dream of the Kingdom of God:

    for in the wilderness shall waters break out, and streams in
    the desert. And the parched ground shall become a pool, and
    the thirsty land springs of water.

10. PLAYING IT BY EAR

Just south of the Al Aqsa Mosque and Solomon's stables, and outside the old walls of Jerusalem, is the Pool of Siloam. This pool is famous because of the incident recorded by St John, of a man who had been blind from his birth. His condition became the subject of discussion among the disciples, who were conscious of a theory that incapacity of any kind is the result of sin somewhere along the line. Naturally they put the question to Jesus, 'Master, who did sin, this man or his parents, that he was born blind?' Jesus gave them the straightforward answer, 'Neither hath this man sinned, nor his parents: but that the works of God should be made manifest in him.' Our Lord went on to demonstrate the works of God by anointing the man's eyes with clay and telling him to 'Go, wash in the pool of Siloam.' St. John points out that Siloam means Sent. When the man carried out the instructions his sight was restored.

As the pool stands today, it can scarcely be described as impressive. After descending a flight of steps we stood on a narrow ledge and looked down into shallow water where a number of Arab children were paddling. Any thoughts of stooping down and quenching the thirst were abandoned immediately. The water is far from pure. Nonetheless the Pool of Siloam rouses the spirit of adventure in those who may be young in years or youthful of heart. The pool emerges from a dark tunnel, and this happens to be Hezekiah's tunnel, discovered by an Arab boy and authenticated by an inscription in Phoenician-Hebrew which describes the cutting of the tunnel by miners who worked from end to end, in the hope of meeting in the middle. This they managed to do. Here we were, standing and looking at the entrance to the tunnel. It connects the Gihon spring to the Pool of Siloam and involves a distance of 1700 feet.

The reason for its existence goes back to the early eighth century B.C.,when Jerusalem was in a precarious position at the hands of the Assyrians. These ancient enemies of Israel had already overrun Samaria in the year 721 B.C., and the only way Hezekiah could buy time and postpone the evil day was to pay tribute money to the Assyrian leader, Sennacherib, who

was blockading Jerusalem. This transaction took place in 701
B.C. Simultaneously Hezekiah decided to strengthen his
position by making sure of water supplies while under siege.
Accordingly, he organised two sets of workers, one beginning
at the Gihon spring and the other at the Pool of Siloam so that
the waters were diverted from Gihon into the fortified city. This
extraordinary feat of engineering denied priceless water to the
besiegers and provided for the needs of the besieged. The
indications are that time was of the essence and the workmen
took the risk of getting on to the job right away with haste.
There was no time to survey and trace the course in the modern
way but they decided to play it by ear. This could be said
literally, because as they moved along underground, each party
was guided by the hammering of the other. It is hard to imagine
that the entrance now is the token of a drama which took place
roughly twenty eight centuries ago.

Inevitably this tunnel rouses the sense of adventure in many
who feel the challenge to investigate its dark length and keep
company with the spirits of the workers of the ancient past. In
our party we had an assortment of people of all ages, including
teenagers and others who still regarded themselves as youthful.
These two elements combined their resources and arranged for
a conquering of the hidden mysteries of the tunnel. Since water
still runs through it they decided on bathing togs as the most
suitable clothing. If you would like to go with them in spirit you
can imagine a narrow, dark tunnel with brownish water
snaking along between clammy walls. Sometimes there is
adequate head space and at other times the roof presses down
close enough to cause a certain nervous tension for anyone
inclined to claustrophobia. Hezekiah's workmen were sparing
on height and width for the obvious reasons of economy in time
and labour. The zigzag patterns here and there suggest that the
men had stopped to listen to the tappings of their fellows
working from the opposite direction, so that from time to time
the line of the tunnel had to be corrected. Accordingly this
passage-way linking the Pool of Siloam and the Gihon spring
(or the Virgin's Fountain) speaks of the fears and anxieties of
human beings in the passing centuries, and the frantic efforts
they had to exert in the interests of self-preservation.

Bethesda and Siloam were only two parts of the water supply
of ancient Jerusalem. Solomon's Pools, situated roughly twelve
miles south of Jerusalem and about seven miles beyond

Bethlehem, are set in the midst of a fertile area terraced with vines. There are three pools contained in large stone cisterns formed with geometrical precision. The impression these reservoirs give is of vast bathing pools, an upper, a middle and a lower. The dimensions of the upper are 380 by 230 by 25 feet; the middle 423 by 230 by 39 feet and the lower 582 by 175 by 50 feet. Fed by perennial springs, they lie on the edge of a hill which slopes down into a fertile valley, which is a contrast to the barren hills, a valley which contains traces of ancient orchards and gardens, a valley of fruit trees, waterfalls and fountains. One is reminded of the passage of Scripture in Ecclesiastes, 'I made me great works; I builded me houses; I planted me vineyards; I made me gardens and orchards, and I planted trees in them of all kinds of fruits: I made me pools of water, to water therewith the wood that bringeth forth trees.'

Although we were conscious of Nature's generosity in this corner of the Holy Land, of the ancient water supply, of the everlasting springs (providential as they are) yet it was a human encounter which touched our hearts most and embedded itself in our minds. While looking at the reservoirs we became aware we were not standing alone, my wife and I. An old Arab had shuffled into our company from nowhere. His swarthy face was wrinkled, and he had a questioning yet hopeful look in his deep-set eyes as he watched for our reaction to him. He could not speak English, nor could we use Arabic. However, with friendly gestures and smiles we gained some rapport. He obviously wanted some help but was searching his mind as to how to go about the quest. My wife offered him a coin which he accepted as if it were treasure. He made the gestures of thanks and appreciation. Then he began to search through his garments. It was clear he wished to give us something in return. Eureka! He found something — a single olive about the size of a large, black grape and of the same colour! He handed it to my wife with expansive smiles, and she returned the compliment by accepting it as if it were treasure too — and in a way it was. We felt warmed by the transaction, as the old man went happily on his way.

11. THE HOUSE OF BREAD

There is still much to be seen and considered in Jerusalem, both in the old city and the new, but since many of these sites are associated with the dramatic trial and death of our Lord we leave them while we follow events elsewhere, and return to Jerusalem later. So we go south and take a short journey of six miles to Bethlehem, the birthplace of our Lord. As we have seen, the name of Bethlehem is made up of two Hebrew words — Beth and lehem — which translated means 'The house of bread.' So in the House of Bread was born He who said: 'I am the bread of life.' Bethlehem is also the birthplace of our Lord's royal ancestor, King David, in whose honour it was called 'royal David's city.'

The Christmas story over the years has cast such a spell in the heart of Christians, with the joyous carols, happy scriptural readings, wholesome fellowship, peace and goodwill, that there is bound to be an exciting sense of anticipation as we follow the invitation of the shepherds of the Gospel records, 'Let us now go even unto Bethlehem, and see this thing which is come to pass, which the Lord hath made known unto us.' Here is the cradle of the Kingdom of God and of the Divine mind, heart and intention. Here is the humble manger whence came the call to reconciliation between man and God, man and his fellows and a man and himself, derived from the redeeming power of the love of God. In utter simplicity and humble setting, Bethlehem and all for which it stands is bound to captivate the human soul from generation to generation till the end of time

As we approach the town we are reminded of the words of our Lord that 'a city set on a hill cannot be hid.' For Bethlehem is set on a hill. At one time it stood on the side of the hill, looking down on the valleys below and out towards the arid Judaean hills and beyond to the Dead Sea and the purple hills of Moab. During the years, however, the buildings have sprawled over the hill on every side, developing into a wide urban complex. The predominant colour of the masonry is white, so that one carries in the mind a bright impression of a white town reflecting the light of the sunshine. Above the square and the rectangular buildings rise the bell towers and a few minarets,

for Bethlehem is chiefly inhabited by Christians. As our bus
grinds to a halt one belfry in particular draws our attention —
the one associated with the Church of the Nativity, the bells of
which ring out on Christmas Eve to herald the dawn of
Christmas Day, and which are heard throughout the world on
radio and television.

This would be a good point at which to pause, to set at rest the
minds of those who feel a little dissatisfied at what they may
see at the sacred sites. When you pick up a visitor's guide to the
Holy Land, you find that churches have been built over and
around the holy places. So much thought and devotion have
been put into the construction of these churches that they have
become an attraction in themselves. In Bethlehem, for
instance, the Roman, the Greek and the Armenian Churches
have a stake in the area of the Nativity, and it follows that each
in its reverence has brought to bear its own influence. The
result is that some may feel that the visible church has taken
away the original simplicity of the New Testament events and
imposed something of itself. It is easier to adapt oneself to the
environment if two things are borne in mind. These churches
are regarded as places of pilgrimage and are intended to help
the devotional and meditative heart to relate to the event that
once took place in an unadorned rural setting. The churches
also afford a protection for the sites themselves and over a
period of centuries they have served the valuable function of
preservation. The mosaic illustrations are an artistic
expression of the event associated with that particular place. It
is therefore open to every visitor to see there what he wants to
see, and to look beyond all the human expressions of devotion
and adoration into the heart of the event itself. For some it
means making use of the gift of abstraction, and why not! The
second point to bear in mind is that the sacred sites are often
arrived at by going down a series of steps. The reason is logical.
Two thousand years have passed since Jesus was born in
Bethlehem of Judaea, and the debris of centuries gathers and
mounts inevitably until it is necessary to excavate carefully to
find the original. One goes down steps to the cave of the
Nativity, to Jacob's well and to the tomb of Lazarus. Having
said this we approach the Church of the Nativity.

Alighting from the bus we found ourselves standing in an
open space, called Manger Square. Although it was not the
market day some of the country folk were to be seen with a few

goats, sheep, donkeys, mules and the odd camel. The local people were dressed in a mixture of eastern and European style — young men wearing the familiar long trousers, open-neck shirt and short burnous, older men clad in longer robes, and the women in the usual national costume we have come to associate with the Holy Land. In a colourful way they set the stage for our visit to the Church of the Nativity, said to stand over the place where Jesus was born.

This Church is no doubt the oldest monument of Christian architecture in the world. It was built by the Roman Emperor Constantine, very likely at the suggestion of his mother Helena, who, when she became a Christian, took an obsessive interest in the sacred places and sought to preserve them. The construction of the building began in the year A.D. 326, and a renovation was undertaken by Justinian around A.D. 571. It has survived the numerous invasions of the country, and even the holocaust of Persian destruction which levelled so many of the Christian edifices in A.D.611. Throughout the centuries, renovation and restoration have been necessary, but the ancient stonework still preserves the sense of historic roots. The roof and floor have been renewed frequently. The repair of the former, in the year A.D. 1480 was facilitated by the gift of timber from Philip, Duke of Burgundy, and a further present of lead from King Edward IV of England. Below the present floor are remains of the original fourth-century mosaic floor, which seems to have been the popular style adopted by the early Christians. Another example of elaborate mosaic flooring from the third century can be seen near The Lake of Galilee which we will consider later.

As we approach the entrance of the Church, we can see clearly that the small door is only a fraction of the size it once was. It is easy to discern that the original entrance has been bricked up, leaving this small aperture which forces the question, 'Why?' Our Arab guide offered us three reasons and left it to ourselves to make the choice. The first reason is that the reduced size of the door made it easier to keep out the animals which were inclined to wander in from the nearby market place. Secondly it gave protection from invading enemies on horseback, who felt it a privilege to show their contempt by riding mounted through the nave. It is the third reason which is most appealing. Every person must go through this small door to make their way to the cave where Jesus was

born. Of necessity one must bow low to go in, and so, in a
symbolic way, show a sense of reverence and devotion. Each of
these suggestions arouses further thoughts. One supposes that
the animals we love were never far away when Jesus came into
our world. One likes to think that some things in life are sacred
and have to be protected from the thoughtlessness of the
secular. We can never meditate upon the manger without
hearing in the deep places of the soul, the words of the
Christian hymn:

O come, let us adore Him, Christ the Lord.

Once through the entrance, we straighten up and find ourselves
in a plain, austere building styled on the Roman basilica. The
roof is supported by about fifty Corinthian pillars of polished
red Bethlehem limestone. Since there are so many of these
columns, it is assumed that they belong to Justinian's
reconstruction rather than to Constantine's original building.
Patches of mosaic decoration on the north and south walls of
the nave are deemed to be the work of the twelfth century.

When visiting this Church for the first time, the anticipation
of going down to the cave means that the Church itself is
something like a curtain-raiser to the main purpose of the visit,
so we do not pursue the historical quest with the concentration
it deserves.

At the crossing of the transepts the cave of the Nativity may
be approached from two stairways, one to the north and the
other to the south. This arrangement is attributed to the work of
the Crusaders. Once at the bottom of the stairs, we enter the
cave, the walls of which are partly masonry and partly rock.
The marble facing will strike many as artificial, especially
when they meditate upon what the original scene must have
been when Mary gave birth to her first-born son. Inside the
cave is a little niche, where a silver star is embedded upon the
floor with the Latin inscription, 'Here Jesus Christ was born of
the Virgin Mary', with the date 1717. So recent a date reminds
us that a star similar to this one was stolen in 1847, and played
a part in causing the conflict in the Crimea between France and
Russia. The present star was a replacement in 1852.

Down three more steps on the south side of the cave is a rock
ledge, the site of the manger. It is difficult to describe one's
thoughts and feelings on seeing it. To summon up a response
from your soul that would be adequate to the occasion and the
event that took place when 'the fulness of the time' had come,

seems impossible. Thought is suspended and emotion confused, but pent up feelings were released when the assembled party, simultaneously and in utter sincerity, sang the simple hymn:

Away in a manger, no crib for a bed,
The little Lord Jesus laid down His sweet head.
The stars in the bright sky looked down where He lay,
The little Lord Jesus asleep in the hay.

As we sang each line of the hymn, which we knew by heart, all man-made efforts to do honour to the site faded and we were in heart and thought among the simple and unadorned surroundings of the first Christmas. It was a few minutes in a lifetime which I will never forget. On our way out of the Church of the Nativity, we looked up once again at the belfry to catch a glimpse of the bells which would continue to ring out at Christmas. They will be cherished for ever as a symbol of joy.

12. THE SHEPHERDS' FIELDS

From the Church of the Nativity it is just a short walk to the fields so romantically associated with the Christmas theme. Down the slope on the right (on the eastern side of Bethlehem) we came to the Shepherds' Fields. Hereabouts the shepherds were keeping watch over their flocks by night when they heard of the wonderful event, 'For unto you is born this day in the city of David, a Saviour, which is Christ the Lord. And this shall be a sign unto you; ye shall find the babe wrapped in swaddling clothes, lying in a manger.... Glory to God in the highest, and on earth peace, goodwill towards men'.

Standing on the grass and looking around we could easily imagine the events of that first Christmas. In the surrounding pastures we could see the flocks of sheep and the herds of goats, the olive trees scattered around, affording shelter for the animals in the heat of the day, and the limestone caves which served, also, as shelter from the elements. These caves were again useful when the shepherds wished to guard their flock from possible attack by wild animals. They could be assembled within the caves and the shepherds themselves would take up sentinel duty at the entrances. Farther down the valley were fields of wheat and barley and terraced vineyards at various levels on the slopes. A young shepherd, in his native costume, passed by us with a flock of sheep and goats, and though far removed from them by the centuries, his appearance linked him with the ancient ancestors of his calling. Part of the shepherd's equipment is the pastoral pipe, which the shepherd lad can make for himself out of reeds. It is composed of two reeds, with holes for fingering like our tin whistle, and there are two mouth pieces which give a reasonable range to the adept. It is easy to conclude that these shepherd boys are skilled in playing, since theirs is a lonely job at times, and they have ample opportunity to practise and thus pass more pleasantly the uneventful spells.

How romantic are the incidents associated with the land on which we were standing and at which we were looking on every side! Here we recall the fascinating story surrounding Ruth,

who married one of the sons of Elimelech and Naomi. The
family had travelled east to Moab because there was a famine
in their own land. When they had settled into Moabite country,
their sons Mahlon and Chilion married locally Orpah and
Ruth. Then tragedy struck with the death of the father and both
sons. Feeling the loneliness of her position, Naomi decided to go
back to Bethlehem, and tried to dissuade Orpah and Ruth from
joining her, believing it would be better for them to stay in
Moab, their homeland. Orpah was persuaded but not so Ruth.
Her words of love and devotion must be immortal, 'Do not urge
me to go back and desert you. Where you go, I will go, and
where you stay, I will stay. Your people shall be my people, and
your God, my God. Where you die, I will die, and there will I be
buried. I swear a solemn oath before the Lord your God:
nothing but death shall divide us.'

In time, her loyalty was richly rewarded. In Bethlehem she
was noticed by Boaz, a kinsman of the late Elimelech, and he
undertook to marry Ruth, with her consent. They had a son
called Obed. Obed had a son called Jesse, and Jesse had a son
called David, that sweet Psalmist of Israel and ancestor of our
Lord. So Bethlehem links these romantic events together.

Here we also recall the great confrontation between David,
the shepherd boy of Israel and the giant Goliath, the warrior of
the Philistines. Since the story is so well known it is not
necessary to tell it here. Yet as we look down into the valley we
are conscious of the youthful contender's words: 'Thou comest
to me with a sword, and with a spear, and with a shield: but I
come to thee in the name of the Lord.'

Although the staff of Goliath's spear was like a weaver's
beam, the spear's head proportionately heavy, and he was
strongly protected with armour, he had no chance of coming to
grips with this stripling who relied on his own weapon, the
sling.

In Bethany we were approached by a young Arab who was
selling pipes and slings, and I bought one of each. I am glad
that I did, because they have become, for me, symbols of
Bethlehem. At that time, I asked the young vendor how David
could have killed a giant with what looked to be a
comparatively inoffensive weapon. An older Arab noticed the
questioning and joined us. 'Let him see you use it!' he
suggested. The younger man looked round to see in which
direction he could cast the stone without causing some hurt or

damage, and decided on an open field nearby. Putting a stone
in the sling, he wound it round and round till he was satisfied
he had reached the point of release, and it shot into the distance
like a silent bullet from a gun. It was difficult to believe that
this weak little sling made of goat and camel hair could produce
such power and effect.

'How far can you sling a stone?' I followed up.

'Half a mile!' he said, without hesitation. 'David — he use a
sling like this. He practise well every day as a shepherd boy. He
take five stones to fight Goliath. He only need one.'

So somewhere out there in the valley near the Shepherds'
Fields and close to Bethlehem, David took a smooth stone from
the brook and saved Israel from the hands of the Philistines by
killing their champion, as once he had successfully killed a lion
and a bear.

Finally, here in Bethlehem, we realise we are standing at the
point where our Christian faith was cradled. In lowly
circumstances and environment, in utter simplicity and
humble conditions, a little child was born who has presented
the world with the probing principles of the Sermon on the
Mount; the deep compassion of one who wanted those who
laboured and were heavy laden to find rest and strength in
Him. Born in a manger Himself, because there was no room for
Him in the inn, He provided for the multitude of poor and
hungry, bread enough and to spare. In an environment charged
with political tension and fettered by prejudice He proclaimed
the glorious liberty of the sons and daughters of God. One born
to be king has set before humanity a kingdom that knows no
frontiers in time or space. As one takes a parting look at
Bethlehem, one is convinced that His divine patience must
eventually be rewarded, that He will see of the travail of His
soul and be satisfied. The influence and power of that life which
began in Bethlehem and continues forever in spite of Calvary,
remains to be born anew in those who respond to Him. Still He
makes Bethlehem and the faith for which it stands 'the house
of bread'. To come to Him is never to hunger and to believe in
Him is never to thirst.

13. THE FRIEND

Travelling south and a little to the west of Bethlehem we come to the town of Hebron, a city which, along with Damascus, can claim to be one of the oldest of the world. It was built around 1730 B.C., and is the place to which Abraham came when he crossed over from Mesopotamia into the land of Canaan. Here took place the events recorded in the Patriarchal section of the book of Genesis. This area was a pivot around which Abraham organised the transition from the nomadic life to a more settled existence. With the increase of his flocks and herds, a growing family and spreading household, it became necessary for him and Lot, his brother, to separate, the latter going to the cities of the plain and Abraham remaining in the hill country. It was from this place that Abraham planned the campaign against Chedorlaomer, who had invaded the Dead Sea country and taken Lot captive. Abraham pursued his enemy, who had journeyed north, and rescued his brother.

This is not the place to examine the history which involves the name of Abraham with Hebron, but it is interesting to note some of the events which occurred in the Patriarch's time, and which are reflected in Hebron today. It will be recalled that Abraham had a child by Hagar, an Egyptian handmaid to his wife Sarah, and with the latter's consent. At the time, Sarah was concerned because she was barren. The name of the child was Ishmael, and he later became a figure in the Arab world. Soon afterwards Sarah did have a child, Isaac, who carried on the lineage of Abraham through Jacob. These links with the distant past are represented to-day in the ancient mosque Al-Harem Al-Ibrahimi where, under a common roof, Jew, Moslem and Christian find religious ties. Both Moslems and Jews hold services within this ancient building periodically, and one hopes that, given time, the family ties of ancient days may become a reconciling force in the land. There is certainly no indication in the Bible record of bitterness and hostility between Abraham and the Hittites among whom he had come to dwell. We read that 'Sarah died in Kirjath-Arba; the same is Hebron in the land of Canaan.' Although living in the area, Abraham had no place to bury his dead, so he approached the sons of Heth, 'I am a stranger and a sojourner with you: give me a possession of a burying place with you.' The reply was most gracious and couched in the courteous language of the east: 'Hear us, my Lord; thou art a mighty prince among us; in the choice of our sepulchres bury thy dead; none of us shall withold from thee his sepulchre, but that thou mayest bury thy dead.' Abraham was deeply touched, and mentioned the cave of Machpelah as a possible purchase. This cave belonged to one called Ephron, to whom Abraham offered whatever money it was considered to be worth. At the gate of the city where such transactions generally took place, Ephron stated in the presence of his brethren, 'Nay, my Lord, hear me; the field give I thee, and the cave that is therein, I give it thee; in the presence of the sons of my people give I it thee: bury thy dead.'

Abraham, however, while appreciating the gesture, wanted to pay for the field and the cave, and eventually Ephron agreed to the offer by saying: 'The land is worth four hundred shekels of silver; what is that betwixt me and thee? Bury thy dead.'

So Abraham purchased the property for the price suggested, and the relationships between Abraham and the Hittites certainly seem to have been most cordial. The mosque has been built shadowing Machpelah, and attendants guard with devotion the tomb in which the remains of Abraham and his nearest and dearest lie. The six large cenotaphs are said to stand directly over their respective graves, Abraham and Sarah's holding the central position with Isaac and Rebekah, Jacob and Leah on either side. A little distance away, but still linked with the group, is the resting place of Joseph, because it is generally thought that he had this place in mind when he spoke to his kindred in his dying words, — 'God will surely visit you, and bring you out of this land (Egypt) unto the land which He sware to Abraham, to Isaac and to Jacob.... Ye shall carry up my bones from hence.' We read that they embalmed him, no doubt with the intention of taking his remains to the family burying place.

Leading to the cave are two passages which speak of ancient days, when the Canaanites and the nomads who had come from the other side of the Euphrates lived in concord. When we think of Leah we also think of Rachel who died on the way to Bethlehem when giving birth to Benjamin, and was buried between Jerusalem and Bethlehem. Abraham is known as 'the friend of God and the father of the faithful,' and Hebron means 'the alliance'. The modern Arab name is Al-Khalil which means 'The Friend' so we pray that the spirit of friendship may grow and prosper in Hebron as it did in ancient days.

A second link with the ancient past is that Hebron lies in the luxuriant valley of Eshcol which has been famous for centuries for its juicy grapes, its olives, apricots, nuts, figs and pomegranates. We read in the thirteenth chapter of the Book of Numbers that Moses sent spies out to discover what the land of Canaan was like before making an invasion. His instructions were, 'See the land, what it is; and the people that dwelleth therein, whether they be strong or weak, few or many; And what the land is that they dwell in, whether it be good or bad; and what cities they be that they dwell in, whether in tents or in strongholds.'

Travelling up from the south, they came to Hebron. Adventuring through the valley of Eshcol, they reached the brook. After a period of forty days' investigation they returned to their camp, bringing with them a glowing report. They had cut down a cluster of grapes, and carried back with them pomegranates and figs as samples of the fertility and fruit of the land. 'Surely it floweth with milk and honey; and this is the fruit of it.'

The modern pilgrim is conscious of the richness of the valleys in the neighbourhood of Hebron, for the city is a market place today for the same exotic fruits, and the vendors need no encouragement. No sooner had we stepped down from the bus than a wave of youthful and enthusiastic merchants literally forced their wares upon us. Those who sold fur hats of various shapes would set one upon your head and have you buy it, like it or not. These hustling salesmen were overpowering in their exuberance, and it was with a sense of relief that we escaped to make our way safely to a nearby shop and found sanctuary where the horde oppressing us were not allowed to enter.

We found ourselves in a shop like an Aladin's cave with rows upon rows of shelves on every side filled with glass-ware, pottery, and wooden ornaments made from the popular olive wood. Draped here and there, in artistic array, were samples of heavily embroidered cloth. I remember being intrigued by a little girl of nine years of age, who was painting designs on cups and vessels prior to glazing. Her young, artistic hand held the brush with sureness as she painted a ring of flowers with complete confidence, apparently not allowing the thought to enter her head that she could possibly make a mistake. This seemed all the more remarkable, considering that so many people were watching her at her work.

Hebron is a hive of industry where many forms of craft are practised. One of these is the making of glass-ware. Passing along a street, one can see, through the open doorway of a shop, the glow of a furnace and the figures of men and boys engaged in glass-blowing, thrusting long rods into the molten glass, and creating a variety of intricate and beautiful shapes which are finished off as vases, jugs or bottles even while you wait.

If you look through another door you can become fascinated by the potter working the clay on his wheel. They make their ornaments so easily, it is evident that the craft has been handed down with local expertise from generation to generation. In yet another place the tanner is busy, and elsewhere other deft hands are engaged in the manufacture of sacking and other finer materials.

Finally, we recall that Hebron was once the capital city of Judaea, and that King David lived here for seven years before conquering Jerusalem which subsequently replaced Hebron as capital. We also remember it was at Hebron that Abner became the victim of Joab's ambition when the general slew him at the gate of the city. At the funeral David himself followed the bier, and both he and the people wept. It was also just outside the gate that David executed the murderers of Ish-bosheth, the son of Saul. Here Absalom organised a revolt against his father David and sent spies through all the tribes of Israel saying, 'As soon as ye hear the sound of the trumpet, then shall ye say, Absalom reigneth in Hebron.'

The revolt failed, and perhaps no more touching words are to be found than those of King David when he learned of the death of his rebellious son, and wept sore:'O my son Absalom, my son, my son Absalom! would God I had died for thee, O Absalom, my son, my son!'

Once out in the wide square again we take a parting glance at the Harem el Khalil, this imposing work of Herod the Great in its monumental enclosure; at the huge blocks of stonework reminiscent of the platform of the temple at Jerusalem, and wonder what it would have been like if the Crusaders had been in the position to stay there in the twelfth century. For a season Hebron had a bishop, but his presence was short-lived because the Moslems took over in A.D. 1187. No drama could be more

colourful than that which has been part of the everyday
experience of Hebron, as one traces these events into the mists
of the distant past. Hebron may truly be regarded as the Friend,
since, from the days of Abraham, three of the world's greatest
religions hold the city in reverence; the Jews, the
Mohammedans and the Christians.

14. DOWN JERICHO WAY

Every traveller to Israel knows in his heart that there is a journey he must take, and that is the road from Jerusalem to Jericho. It is a road that has been immortalised by our Lord's matchless parable of the Good Samaritan. Jesus Himself knew the Jericho road well and the people to whom He told the parable were very familiar with it too. Once we become acquainted with the road, we sense how the story pulsates with life. This parable has been examined so closely, and written about so profusely that I only wish to touch upon the sentence which is related to the nature of the journey. The parable begins: 'A certain man went down from Jerusalem to Jericho.' On a casual reading we may think little about this remark. We could accept it as similar to 'I knew a man who went down to the seaside one day.' The word 'down', however, really means down. Jerusalem is a city set on a hill, and, within the space of roughly twenty-three miles, the road descends through the necessary twists and curves to Jericho, which is the lowest city in the world, being 1300 feet below the level of the sea. If an earthquake were to open a passage through the Judaean hills from Jericho to the Mediterranean, then the Jordan gorge would be flooded and the whole face of the landscape altered beyond all recognition. With Jerusalem standing at roughly 2700 feet above sea level and Jericho at 1300 feet below, the certain man would have gone down about 4000 feet in a journey of twenty-three miles. He would have descended from the normal Middle East temperature of the Holy City to the really hot climate of tropical Jericho. There can scarcely be another road in the world quite like that from Jerusalem to Jericho. A steep road. A twisting road. An inhospitable road.

Once it was dangerous because of the lurking brigands who would assail the unwary traveller and then disappear easily into the hills and ravines to take refuge in hiding places among caves and rocks. The road is still inhospitable because of the wilderness that lines it on each side, offering no respite from a relentless, burning sun. We journeyed by bus, and were thankful for modern methods of transport. For a considerable part of the journey we looked out on tawny, arid hills and bare,

wild, stony ravines. The shimmering heat settled mercilessly
on everything.

About midway on the route, the bus came to a halt to enable
us to visit an ancient khan which is known as the Inn of the
Good Samaritan. It is a one-storey structure like many of the
old Turkish khans, with accomodation for both man and beast.
This one-time resting place is oblong in shape, with the wall of
a substantial courtyard protruding to the rear and forming a
protected area against the wilderness which surrounds it on all
sides. In the centre of the long wall is the entrance, a high
arched doorway. An indication of the antiquity of the site is the
floor of the original inn which stands excavated for all to see,
and below are the old rock cisterns which were probably made
by the Romans before our Lord's time.

Our visit was enhanced by the presence of an Arab in full
costume, together with his camel, also traditionally draped in
its brightly coloured accoutrements. Two of his children,
similarly dressed for the occasion, were close at hand, ready to
be photographed for a 'consideration'. Many of us were glad to
have a picture of this colourful reminder of our visit to the Inn
of the Good Samaritan.

Just as we realised that it was time to move on to the next
stage of our journey, a scene developed in front of us so
unexpected, unrehearsed and surprising that we had to see it
through its full sequence. On one of the rounded hills directly in
front of the inn, the lone figure of an Arab came slowly into
view. He was dressed in national costume so that he might
have been emerging out of Bible times. We saw him
immediately, because any moving thing was bound to draw
attention in the otherwise still landscape. Then we noticed that
he was not alone but was the leader in what turned out to be a
slow procession. Behind him followed a flock of sheep and a
herd of goats. Each species moved in its own group and
provided an animate study in black and white. Slowly the
procession moved across the face of the hill, the animals with
their heads down in the manner of grazing. They never
stopped, but moved very slowly behind the shepherd who led
the way. The puzzling thing to us was — what were they
eating? Not a blade of grass was to be seen, or vegetation of any
kind. So we turned to our Arab guide, and sought an
explanation.

'You see no green grass at present because it is all withered

up by the sun. When the rain comes in Spring, the grass grows.
When the grass withers the roots are still there. The sheep and
the goats are nibbling at the roots of the grass. When the rains
come again in Autumn, the grass grows green and the process
goes on.

You know the difference between a wilderness and a desert?
Yes? No?' He could see we were waiting for an answer.

'The wilderness has potential life and will blossom if it gets
water, but the desert will not. This part of the hills is just
wilderness as you look at it now, but when the rains come, the
shepherd leads the sheep and goats through green grass
instead of dry roots.'

We took one more glance at the shepherd and his flock. As
they disappeared round to the other side of the hill we realised
that we had just been witnessing a scene from St John's Gospel.

Our next stop was a brief one, to take a photograph of a large
wooden signboard set up to mark sea level. We knew that from
this point we were descending below the level of the
Mediterranean and going deeper and deeper into the Jordan
Gorge. Down the circuitous road we journeyed, on a good
surface which would have seemed marvellous to travellers in
the first century who had to be content with the dusty track. We
were still descending into the gorge when, on rounding a bend,
we saw the Dead Sea. It was surrounded by a ring of green, in
the midst of the tawny wilderness. Eventually we found
ourselves travelling on the level plain of Jericho. We were in a
tropical area where we saw rows and rows of banana trees,
together with all the other fruits which have been associated
with Jericho, oranges, melons, pomegranates, dates and figs.

As we eagerly awaited our arrival at the Dead Sea our Guide
talked about Israel's modern 'Kibbutzim'. These are
communities of Jewish people who have come from different
parts of the world with the high hopes of finding a new life
where they could feel at home in their own traditions. Coming
from Germany, Russia, America, and some of the smaller
countries of Europe they are gradually establishing
themselves. Here in tropical heat they have settled for a life
where each is for all and all for each. They are farming the land
and building for the future. Together they face the struggles to
win over nature and to feel secure in their togetherness. In this
way they are sure of a roof over their heads, work to do, and the
inspiration of a common objective.

Soon the bus reduced its pace and drew to a halt at a T junction. When we alighted, we found ourselves at a point where we could either turn to the right hand or to the left. The left led to old Jericho and the right to the modern town. The reason for our stop, however, was not the decision as to whether to go to old or new, but to look at a tremendous tree with a huge trunk and massive foliage spreading out from quite low down in the trunk in every direction. Your guess would be right - the sycamore tree which Zacchaeus climbed when he wanted to see Jesus 'who He was' as the Lord was entering Jericho.' Could it be the same tree?' we asked. Well, it is definitely an ancient tree, judging by the massive width of the trunk, and it has been associated with the name of the New Testament tax-gatherer for centuries. If it is not the same tree, its position would strongly suggest that it is a successor. Two phrases kept running through my mind as I looked at the old yet flourishing tree — the words of Zacchaeus, 'Behold Lord, the half of my goods I give to the poor; and if I have taken anything from any man by false accusation, I restore him fourfold', and the words of Jesus,'This day is salvation come to this house.'

Modern Jericho lives up to its name, 'the city of palm trees.' The trees lend beauty to the whole layout. The flowers and shrubs of the gardens fill the environment with colour, and the atmosphere with fragrance. However, our main objective was to visit old Jericho, and so, satisfying ourselves with a short acquaintance with the modern, we turned back to where the excavation of the ancient sites is going on.

Proceeding north of the present town for about one and a half miles we came to a wire-enclosed mound which is adjacent to the excavations of the ancient site of Jericho. In 1907 a German expedition had begun to open up the area under the leadership of Watzinger,and this was followed by more archaeological investigation by a British expedition under Garstang from 1929 to 1936. The labours of these men yielded important finds and, accordingly, we were able to look at a substantial section of an ancient tower estimated to be about 6,000 years old. The rounded walls of mud brick are quite distinct, and their appearance belies their age. We bear in mind that in such dry soil old structures will last almost indefinitely, provided that there is no vandalism. These excavations have revealed a neolithic village that is estimated to date back to 5000 B.C. or earlier, and with it go plaster figures of humans and animals, as well as the usual pottery and flint tools. There followed in chronological succession three cities of the bronze age. Apparently there were but slight traces of habitation in Jericho around 1200 B.C., and whatever inhabitants there were abandoned the site. It remained deserted until it was reoccupied by the Israelites in Ahab's time, about 875 B.C. This was the era of the great prophets Elijah and Elisha.

What attracts the curiosity of the layman is to know whether there are any indications of the remains of the old walls of Jericho which crumbled under the onslaught of Joshua.The experts refer to the evidence of the destruction of a Canaanite city, which would coincide with Joshua's time. Under some violent influence, the walls had collapsed down the slopes of the mound upon which they had been built. There were signs of intense burning. This has led to one of the theories as to what happened when Joshua and his army were advancing into the Promised Land. Taking into consideration the evidence of burning, the suggestion is that an earthquake had destroyed Jericho at the time, and earthquakes are part of the hazards of living in this deep crack on the earth's surface. So the Israelites did not have to attack Jericho, which fell into their hands of its own accord.

Our Arab guide offered to us another ingenious theory. 'You will notice that in Joshua's time the walls were made of hardened mud. While the armies of Israel marched round seven times, the inhabitants stood on the walls, terrorised by the display. Finally when the climax came with the sounding of the trumpets, those who had gathered on the walls rushed to one section to see what was happening, and under their combined weight the walls collapsed and the city fell.'

A third suggestion is linked to the second. It was an example of psychological warfare. Making use of the superior display of manpower and weaponry, Israel chilled the hearts of the inhabitants of Jericho. Accordingly, when they advanced to the assault no resistance was offered and the city surrendered. No doubt many other explanations could be offered, but these were sufficient to whet our curiosity as we looked down a considerable depth to what had been the ground level of former generations of man.

Looking across the Jordan to the east, we could see the mountains of Moab with Pisgah and Nebo in their midst. We thought of Moses standing there after the long journey from

Egypt, being given a glimpse of the dream that had kept him marching without being granted the privilege of entering the land of his dreams. In all human lives many threads are left ungathered while those who follow enter into the fruits of their labours.

From where we stood on the remains of old Jericho we looked northwards into the plain. There we saw quite a sizeable encampment which at first suggested a kibbutz. Our guide told us it was, in fact, an Arab refugee camp and there in twentieth-century starkness we were looking upon the Arab-Israeli problem.

Not too far away and beyond this camp stood a mountain, bare and bleak. This is said to be the Mount of Temptation — the place where our Lord had to endure the particular temptations associated with His Messiahship. There was no sign of verdure anywhere on the mountain, and one can well appreciate the force of the temptation: 'And when He had fasted forty days and forty nights He was afterward hungered. And when the tempter came to him, he said, If Thou be the Son of God, command that these stones be made bread.' But He answered and said, 'It is written, Man shall not live by bread alone, but by every word that proceedeth out of the mouth of the Lord.' Certainly, wherever Jesus looked there were stones in plenty.

From the earthworks of the excavations we crossed to the other side of the highway, and there, in a pleasant little modern cafe, we thoroughly enjoyed a grapefruit drink. It was cool and refreshing and we enjoyed, for a time, a respite from the burning heat of a tropical sun. Nearby, we could hear the sound of running water, which is always music to the ear in any climate, but is especially so in Jericho. Without this water supply, called Elisha's spring, Jericho would scarcely be there in all its rich fertility. This tremendous source of water pours out 140,000 gallons of water every day, and it is the life-blood of the Plain of Jordan.

The next step on our tour took us down to the shores of the Dead Sea. It was the opportunity for a swim, which should be refreshing in the heat of the day. It was, indeed, refreshing up to a point. The water was warm enough to encourage us to bathe as long as the inclination would last, but the novelty soon wore off. Because of the density of the water it was difficult to swim. It was more a question of floundering around. Someone had suggested that we should try to sit on the water and read a newspaper at the same time, but we recognised the suggestion as a leg-pull, since it was obviously impossible to keep one's balance. Added to this inconvenience was the irritation of the little pebbles which were very severe on our feet. Since there are no tides, the rough edges of the stones have not been smoothed, and for anyone with tender feet bathing in the Dead Sea without sandals can be a truly painful process. On returning to the huts where we had undressed, we had to be careful to walk on the wooden planks supplied and avoid the hot sand which could burn the skin.

The water is so laden with chemicals, such as salt (27%), potassium, magnesium and carbon, that it is even more refreshing to have a shower after the bathe to wash away the greasy layer left by the liberally salted water. The reason for the strong chemical content is evaporation. The heat of the sun exhausts 7 million tons of water which flow in each day from the Jordan, and since there is no outlet to the Sea, the chemical content becomes increasingly high. No fish could survive and this has its effect on bird life. No fish — no birds! Hence the name — the Dead Sea.

Those of a theological turn of mind often use the Dead Sea as an illustration. It receives, continually, water from the River Jordan but, unlike the Sea of Galilee, it does not give any out. The inference, when applied to human living, does not need to be stressed. All take and no give is unhealthy. Few analogies, however, are watertight. If, in the past, the Dead Sea was disposed to keep its assets to itself, it is making a better effort now to give the world something in return. Chemical plants have been established and a modern factory is making use of the resources now to be found in this sea.

Further along the coast from where we were bathing are the caves in which the now famous Dead Sea scrolls were found at Qumran. These ancient scripts of part of the Old Testament we were to see later, when, in modern Jerusalem, we were to visit the Shrine of the Book.

15. THE DESCENDING ONE

Having considered the steep descent of the road from Jerusalem to Jericho, we shall now turn in the direction of the River Jordan, whose name means The Descending One. No visitor to Israel can fail to make acquaintance with this famous river, because it confronts us whether we visit the northern regions at Mount Hermon, or the central area of Galilee, or the southern district of Judaea. On its 200 mile course through its gorge, it passes through two lakes, Huleh in the north and then Galilee, and comes to an end in the third, the Dead Sea. It descends from the heights of Mount Hermon to 1,300 feet below sea-level. As the crow flies, it would be a distance of seventy miles, but the actual course, as it curves and meanders, stretches to 200 miles.

The sources of the Jordan are to be found at Mount Hermon, which is over 7,000 feet high and whose snow-capped peak commands the northern boundary of Israel. The two main sources are within easy reach of one another. Four and a half miles lie between Tell-el-Kadi (the mound of the Judge) and Banias. At the foot of the mound, a stream of clear, pure water gushes out, forming the river Hasbany which, in turn, joins the river Banias to form the Jordan. Kadi is the Arab word for the Hebrew Dan, and it is symbolic that the tribe of Dan did not make the same impact in the far north as did the other Hebrew tribes when settling in. The Danites found it easier to mingle with the local inhabitants, and suffered, to some extent, a consequent loss of identity.

As already indicated, the other main source of the Jordan is to be found at the village of Banias. The modern visitor finds himself standing at a fast-flowing stream of clear water, which, in the heat of the foothills around Hermon, tempts the thirsty to stoop down and drink till satisfied. At this point there is a freshness in the water, and a lively music as it gambols along on the first stage of its long journey to the Dead Sea. The stream has already begun to descend with a youthful vitality upon its precipitous way through the gorge which lures it into the depths and finally traps it.

Looking up into the face of a limestone cliff, one can see the large cave which was set apart, in the days of ancient Greece, to the honour of the god Pan, from whom is derived the modern Arabic name of the town. Greek inscriptions still remain. Below this cave, through the debris of rocks and stones, the stream rushes out into a widespread area of parkland and forest. Amidst patches of green turf, gigantic and beautiful trees stand in clumps. A touch of excitement is stirred by bouncing rivulets and waterfalls. As well as the Greek character of the shrine, there are remains of old Roman fortifications, so that the classical civilization impinges upon the twentieth century.

Banias is spelt with a B rather than a P because the Arabs do not use P in their alphabet. The town has been known by different names in its history: it began as Panias, and later became known as Caesarea Philippi, associated with the retreat of our Lord and His disciples when He took them aside to outline the nature of His kingdom and work. For a time it was known as Neroneas in honour of the emperor Nero, and now it has settled down to the Arab name Banias. Apart from the association of the Greek Pan, there is a shrine built by the Arabs on the spot where Herod raised a temple to Augustus, and this shrine honours the name of St George of England. Although he was martyred near Constantinople at the beginning of the fourth century, his name came to be revered throughout the middle East.

From Banias the Jordan runs into a swamp area at lake Huleh. This lake is the 'waters of Merom' of the Old Testament, and is the place where Joshua fought his battle against the kings mentioned in Joshua XI. The swamp is now being drained as part of the new Israel's programme to utilise the precious, reclaimed land. The pressure behind the river soon forces it beyond the small lake as it proceeds towards the south in search of the lake of Galilee. At this point the Descending One is like a runner who starts off strongly and then settles into a slower pace to gain his second wind before achieving a settled rhythm. The Jordan meanders for a time over a broad open plain, adding to the length of its journey. Once it reaches the edge of the plain, the river recovers its earlier *joie de vivre* and gathers speed on the headlong rush for Galilee.

When we visited Capernaum, we had the opportunity of watching the Jordan flow eagerly into the northern part of the lake. We were glad to be able to bathe our hands and sprinkle water on our faces, but we noticed quite a difference in the river from what we had seen at Banias. It was not so clear or so pure. It was dull and muddy, and those of our party who filled a bottle to take home for use at a baptismal font for some friend, remarked upon the amount of sediment. Looking at the river, one realised that the shadow cast by the greenery lining both banks added to the clouded, green-hued appearance of the water. The reason, of course, was the nature of the soil of the river bed over which it had been running. The mud had left its traces. The considerate would say that it was 'clean dirt', but it was not to be drunk just the same. The wealth of foliage on either side of the river reminded me of the Psalmist's reference to 'the tree planted by the rivers of water, that bringeth forth its fruit in its season; his leaf also shall not wither; and whatsoever he doeth shall prosper.'

After reaching the plain, the Descending One enters the lake of Galilee at a point not far from Capernaum. There it mingles to form the soft, mercurial waters of the Lake, which captures such warm thoughts and emotions for the pilgrim. Since it would be better to give to Galilee a window of its own, we will go down to the southern end of the lake where the Jordan emerges once again on the last stage of its journey to the Dead Sea. At this point it is an impetuous stream cutting a deep channel in the yielding soil, often hidden by thick foliage and nourishing tamarisk, oleander and willow.

There was one part of the Jordan which we did not have an opportunity to visit, called the Fords of Jordan. The reason given was that it was not under Israel's jurisdiction at the time. This was the traditional site of our Lord's baptism, when he insisted that John the Baptist 'fulfil all righteousness.' Jesus knew that the time had come for Him to launch forth on the work of the Kingdom, and He identified Himself with all those who were in search of God and had a deep sense of the need of salvation. He was already showing them the way.

The Jordan is not an impressive river either in respect of its length or width, but its geographical setting, its association with the struggles of Israel and the life and work of our Lord have made it the most famous river in the world. The gorge through which it flows is part of a remarkable trench of rift valley which extends across the Levant to the gulf of Aqaba. It also lies in the earthquake belt, and history records landslides in this narrow gorge which have held up the waters on

occasions. The swelling pressure of the rising waters soon
surmounted any barriers and spilled over any obstruction. So
the river ploughed along its chosen course. 'Are not Abana and
Pharpar, rivers of Damascus, better than all the waters of
Israel?' said Naaman the Syrian, when told by Elisha to bathe
in the Jordan in order to cure his leprosy. He was turning away
in a rage when his advisers suggested that he should perform
the simple request. Their wiser counsels prevailed and his flesh
was healed. Muddy and unimpressive this river may be at first
sight, but none can deny the redeeming thoughts that come
teeming into the mind as we stand on the bank and watch the
water flowing by. Symbolically, it is 'de ol' river we long to
cross' when the pilgrimage of life is over.

16. SOUND AND LIGHT

Since the hotel in which we stayed was located on the northern
side of the old city of Jerusalem, we returned there in the
evenings after visiting the many historic and exciting places
within easy reach of the capital. One of the evening
entertainments provided by the city was the event called Sound
and Light. From Herod's Gate we followed the northern wall
past the Damascus Gate and the New Gate, turned the corner
and walked along part of the Jaffa Road till we reached the
Jaffa Gate, which is under the domination of an impressive
stone castle-like structure named the Citadel, or David's Tower.
Its sombre, gaunt towers, suggesting its original function as a
place of defence, stood dimly silhouetted against the night sky,
for the sun had long since gone down. This turreted castle was
constructed on a massive plinth of stonework and is as solid as
a rock. From its foundation platform we entered the David
Garden, and then through an archway into an open courtyard
where, by the help of primitive lighting, we saw rows of chairs
for the benefit of spectators. Once seated, we wrapped rugs
round us to keep us warm in what turned out to be a cool
evening. With a background of music, we chatted among
ourselves till a silence indicated that the programme was about
to begin.

The lighting faded out, and then, quite suddenly, a shaft of
brilliant light penetrated the contrasting darkness and
focussed on a white stone which was presented as a symbol of
David. From that point the programme developed
dramatically, unfolding the story of the growth of the kingdom
of Israel. At relevant focal points, lights of varying colours
illumined the walls in a most impressive way, and the
amplified voices of the characters radiated from various hidden
alcoves in the upper walls of the castle. The sense of drama was
sustained throughout, and the subject matter provided
excellent material for an imposing presentation, especially the
section allotted to the role of Herod the Great.

Herod was an Edomite, but Jewish by religion, who came into
power in Judaea on the collapse of Jewish independence. He
was appointed as an administrator by Julius Caesar in the year

47 B.C., and he and Phasael, his brother, came to share
authority as joint tetrarchs. Both men were deposed, and
replaced in 40 B.C. by Antigonus, a representative of the
Hasmonean dynasty. Phasael committed suicide, and Herod
fled to Rome. The latter was never to forget this insult, as
subsequent events proved. Nor was he going to give up the
struggle for power lightly, for he ingratiated himself with
Antony, under whose patronage his claims were recognised,
and he became tetrarch of Judaea.

When Antony became involved with the Egyptian queen
Cleopatra, he rapidly lost favour at Rome, and in the year 31
B.C. Octavian defeated him at the Battle of Actium. Antony
and Cleopatra committed suicide and Octavian became the
Emperor Augustus Caesar.

Herod entered upon the greatest gamble of his life when, at
this point, he decided to meet Augustus Caesar on the island of
Rhodes, in the hope that he might be allowed to continue in his
own office. Because he had received his position and his
favours from Antony, he was deeply afraid that Augustus
would extend his enmity to him as Antony's puppet. Knowing
full well that he was taking his life in his hands, and afraid lest,
when his own life would be forfeit, his beautiful young wife
Mariamne should become the consort of another man, he left
orders that if he should not return safely she should be put to
death. This decree was to have terrible consequences on his
influence and his character.

His gamble, however, paid off through a bold and resourceful
stroke on his part. He cleverly concealed his fears, and acting
his role superbly, gave Augustus the impression that he was
personally pleased to see him as emperor, and that he himself
had often tried unsuccessfully to persuade Antony to shake off
the tentacles of Cleopatra. So Herod informed Augustus that he
would render the same allegiance to him as he had done to his
predecessor. His service would be faithful. Augustus saw no
reason then to make any change and Herod's genius for
survival prevailed. As a token of goodwill he was granted a
little extra territory.

Once his fears were removed, Herod continued his career. His
public image was impressive and brilliant for a time. He
became a prodigious builder, and was distinguished in his love
for architecture. Under his direction a new temple was erected
in Jerusalem, and he was responsible for the building of cities

like Caesarea and Samaria. Because of his zealous attention to public works, and the tact he showed in naming places in honour of the emperor, his image in Rome was one of an industrious and sophisticated ruler and administrator of the eastern type.

On the other hand he had quite a different reputation at home, where he came to be regarded as an eastern despot of a particularly obnoxious sort. Like a spider, he wove an ever-spreading web of intrigue. His jealousy bred schizophrenic tendencies; his fears, real or imaginary, undermined his judgements and his grasp of reality. He recalled that Antigonus had once ousted him, so he had him murdered along with any of his line who might become a threat to his own position. A morbid suspicion grew like a cancer in his personality, which extended to his nearest and dearest, and many of his relatives were put to death. A whisper reached him that his wife wanted him disposed of, with the result that he struck first and had her assassinated along with two of her sons. No sooner had he taken the tragic step than he was overwhelmed by a morbid remorse, and he drifted in and out of mental disorder with sickening melancholy and with increasing frequency. Mariamne's ghost haunted him till the end of his life.

This was one of the most dramatic moments in the programme that night, the anguished voice of the heart-sick Herod, and the haunting voice of the ghost of Mariamne. No one could have wished to be Herod the Great, for he was possessed of a soul torn apart by love and jealousy, murder and butchery, inhabited by dreams and images of stabbings, stranglings and poisonings. His life was stained with cruelties and atrocities. No one was safe whom he considered to be a hindrance. His hand struck at the Sanhedrin, at court officials, at his mother-in-law, and he framed the decree which caused the slaughter of little children in an effort to put to death the child who was born to be King of the Jews. Half Jew and half Gentile, Herod ended up by being detested in his own kingdom, and although his territories exceeded those of Saul and David, his people yearned for his death. On the other hand, in Rome he continued to be admired to the last for the Romans gave little heed to his atrocities which seemed to be directed more against his own kith and kin. It is said that as death approached, he asked for a knife and an apple. He plunged the knife into his heart, and so, with a dramatic flourish, he merged into history.

As the programme came to an end we were conscious of the relics of Herod's better nature, which he expressed in constructive and progressive work; the tower of Phasael in honour of his brother, who had shared with him the tetrarchy for a short time; the tower in honour of Mariamne, the wife he truly loved, but whom in the madness of jealousy he murdered; and the third tower, sometimes referred to as Hippicus. Herod had also a warm place in his heart for his half-brother Philip whose wife he eventually married, and as a consequence drew upon himself the condemnation of John the Baptist. The 'fire-brand of the desert' felt the sting of Herod's revenge when, at the request of Salome (prompted by her mother Herodias), his head was demanded on a charger. The citadel is alive with dramatic memories, thoughts and suggestions, and is in many ways a symbol of the grandeur and turbulence of Israel's chequered history.

17. KING SOLOMON'S QUARRIES

When young, we loved to read tales of imagination and
adventure, and when older, we sometimes recall the sense of
wonder and excitement these stories fostered within us. The
thought of visiting King Solomon's Quarries sparked off
nostalgic feelings that it would be wonderful to relive the thrills
of those times in history when King Solomon mobilised all his
resources of men and material, and built a temple of such
splendour that even the Queen of Sheba was awestruck. His
workmen began mining under the old city of Jerusalem, and
the sprawling and deviating mines or caverns remain there
today as the workmen left them so long ago, their task
completed.

The sense of discovery and adventure is heightened by
hearing of an incident which occurred a century ago. It tells of a
Dr. Barclay, an American physician, who in 1874 took his two
sons and his dog for a walk along the northern side of the old
city wall. They had just reached the Damascus Gate when the
dog showed some excitement. He had caught the scent of foxes,
and with his hunting instinct on fire, he began to dig eagerly at
a particular point at the base of the wall. Soon he had
uncovered an opening in the ground where the soil had yielded
easily, and into the hole he disappeared. One can imagine how
curious the trio felt as they peered into the excavation and tried
to make out what lay beyond. Their curiosity was stimulated,
and sensing the possibility of adventure, they decided to
investigate.

When they had scooped away more soil, they found
themselves standing at the entrance to a cave. Although they
could not penetrate the darkness inside, they sensed they were
on the verge of something enormous. They were on the brink of
an important discovery, and as the news got round, speculation
mounted as to what might be found in the underground caverns
of the old city. Could it be treasure? The Ark of the Covenant? It
was bound to be something exciting from the past, but who
could tell what?

The doctor arranged a party to explore the cavern, and he
soon discovered that for vastness and intricacy he had never

seen anything like it. With the help of primitive light from
matches and lamps, they saw they were in a cave of
commanding width and height. The ceiling at first seemed to be
supported by massive pillars, but these were not pillars erected
in the ordinary sense. The miners had cut into the face of the
limestone, making extensive holes and opening up new
chambers, but leaving part of the rock untouched in order to
support the ceiling and the weight overhead. This they
discovered to be the general pattern. As they moved into the
interior, one massive section of the cave gave place to another.
So wide-spread did the labyrinth prove to be that the more
imaginative liked to think it was a secret way whereby
one might escape from Jerusalem through a secret exit miles
away. Dr. Barclay had stumbled upon King Solomon's
quarries, and it was indeed a find worthy of all the excitement.
It was evident by the nature of the soil that it had been piled up
by a former generation to conceal the entrance — most likely by
the Turks engaged in the building of the walls in the middle of
the sixteenth century. At any rate, but for a little dog's hunting
instinct, we might not have had the pleasure, even yet, of
visiting King Solomon's Quarries.

Walking by the north wall to see the quarries for ourselves,
we noticed that even today one could easily pass by the
entrance. It is not that it is inadequate, but the attention is
sidetracked to a panorama of brightly coloured flowers growing
in profusion in well-kept beds. This impressive flower garden
blends sweetly with the tawny walls, the stone pavement and
the bright buildings gleaming in the sunlight. Scattered
throughout, at regular intervals, are wooden seats insistently
inviting the pedestrian to sit down, rest awhile and absorb the
benefits of the sun's rays. It was while we were enjoying such a
siesta that we were entertained by tiny lizards which would
cautiously run out from the flower beds, caper for a moment or
two on the pavement and then dart back for cover, no doubt
considering it would be foolhardy to expose themselves for
long.

The entrance to the cave is partially concealed by flowers and
shrubs, but as one draws closer it is quite visible. Once through
the entrance, we found ourselves in an enormous cavern as
large and majestic as a cathedral. It was obvious why the
Arabs call the quarry the 'cotton caves', because the whole
complex is composed of white limestone. Looking here, there

and everywhere, absorbing the historic atmosphere, we walked slowly down into the quarries, following the sloping floor with the help of modern electric lighting which made the going easier than it must have been for former generations of pilgrims, who had to be content to wave lanterns before them and peer ahead in an effort to penetrate the darkness. On either side of the wide ridge along which we walked were deep chasms leading down to other working faces of the quarries. Soon it was obvious that the passages spread out in many directions, and one quarry led to another in labyrinthine style. Without reasonable lighting the adventure would have been fraught with danger, for the rock would suddenly fall away leading to caverns beyond.

As we proceeded in the footsteps of our guide, two main thoughts were in our minds. One related to the times of King Solomon and the other associated with Zedekiah. The uppermost thoughts were with Solomon and the building of the famous temple. The relevant sections of the first Book of Kings tell of the elaborate organisation set up by King Solomon and Hiram, king of Tyre, for its erection in Jerusalem. Hiram undertook to send cedar trees from Lebanon, and to supply skilled men to hew the wood according to necessary specification. Solomon conceded: 'for, as you know, we have none so skilled at felling timber as your Sidonians'.We are then told that great stones, costly stones, and hewed stones should be brought to lay the foundations of the house. Further we read: 'And the house, when it was in building, was built of stone made ready before it was brought thither: so that there was neither hammer nor axe nor any tool of iron heard in the house, when it was in building.'

The impression created by this verse is that the stones were prepared at some distance from the building site, otherwise the sound would have penetrated. Now, as we stood in King Solomon's Quarries, the truth was staring us in the face. Here, right down below the foundations of the old city of Jerusalem, we could not hear a whisper of the heavy traffic which was grinding along outside the entrance. All was silence, and any sound we might make would not penetrate beyond the roof of the caverns, let alone reach the vicinity of the Dome of the Rock where the temple was erected. Yet the distance between the quarries and the building site is comparatively short. King Solomon's workmen could use hammer or axe or any tool of iron, and the sound would never filter beyond this great underground workshop.

The white limestone itself, in its damp raw state, would have been quite easy to shape, and when exposed to the open air it would harden. One can visualise how imposing the brilliant white temple must have looked in its conspicuous setting. Like a city set on a hill, it could not have been hidden. In the quarries themselves, one gets the impression that the walls and excavations stand just as they were when the miners laid down their tools and went home, their task completed. The chippings of the stone lying around are now sometimes used by local artists to fashion souvenirs; there are little niches in the walls where the primitive lamps used to sit so that the workers could do their job. To remove the huge stone slabs of the rock, they first made broad crevices on the wall face and hammered into them wooden wedges. Over these they poured water which caused the timber to swell, and the resulting pressure cracked the stone.

The caves are a famous meeting ground for members of the Masonic Order who regard the builders of the temple as their forbears in office. Members of the Order still hold meetings there, and souvenirs with appropriate symbols find their way to all parts of the world. On the ceiling of one of the caverns is a massive painting of the face of our Lord, which is said to be the work of three Americans who went to explore the complex, lost their way, and have never been seen since.

Although the name of King Solomon comes first to our minds when we think of the quarries, another name is associated with these ancient excavations — Zedekiah. He was the last king of Judah before the conquest of Jerusalem by the Assyrians in the year 587 B.C. In 599 B.C. he was placed on the throne by Nebuchadnezzar and forced to be a tributary of the Babylonian conqueror. This subservience he renounced nine years later, and in order to ward off the Assyrians he allied himself with Egypt. This alliance proved to be a broken reed, because the Egyptians retreated to their homeland without giving battle when confrontation occurred. The Assyrians accordingly were free to besiege Jerusalem, which they did relentlessly till it fell. Zedekiah was taken prisoner and conveyed to Babylon. There he had the cruel experience of witnessing the killing of his two sons before his own eyes were gouged out of their sockets. It is said that a previous attempt at escape by way of the caves during the siege was foiled. The city of Jerusalem was destroyed, the inhabitants captured and the long period of captivity in Babylon commenced.

Branching off from one of the chambers in the quarries is a corridor which leads to a spring where cold and bitter water drips into a basin hewn in the rock. It is called the 'tears of Zedekiah,' in memory of the king's sorrows and his blinding.

The name given to these caverns has changed during the years. Once they were known as 'Zedekiah's Grotto', and then the 'Royal Caverns', and now they are referred to as King Solomon's Quarries. So as we stood in the silence of the underground limestone quarries, we recalled the names of two kings of Israel, the one associated with Israel's glory, the other linked with Israel's defeat when the glory had departed. Fortunately time proved to be the healer, and the exiles of later generations began the trek back.

18. MUST NEEDS GO THROUGH SAMARIA

In our Lord's time, Samaria was sandwiched between Judaea
in the south and Galilee in the north, so when Jesus and His
disciples wished to travel from Galilee to Jerusalem for the
Passover they 'must needs go through Samaria'. The same, of
course, applied to the return journey. We were about to travel
along the same way because the time had come for us to leave
Jerusalem and go north to Nazareth where we were to spend
the second half of our holiday. Jerusalem had been a suitable
headquarters for the explorations not only of the city itself but
also of the surrounding area of Judaea.

Before leaving the city, however, there was one corner we
wished to visit — the sheep market. So, passing by Herod's
Gate and walking east, we found the little cul-de-sac where the
market nestles under the corner of the northern wall. Right
away we were so intrigued by all that was going on that our
cameras became 'click-happy', and were kept busily storing up
scenes to stimulate our memories when Israel would be left far
behind us.

We soon mingled with the Arab shepherds who had taken up
strategic positions in the rectangular, rustic market place.
Around them clustered their sheep and goats, and we enjoyed
being able to draw close enough to the animals to stroke or pat
them. We had seen them at a distance on the slopes of the hills;
it was rewarding to look at them now at close quarters. The
peculiar tails of the sheep were fascinating because each had
the appearance of a small fleece cushion in which they are said
to store up fat and upon which they might be expected to squat
at any moment in the familiar posture of a sitting dog. Huddled
together in their own flocks, they created the impression they
were so tuned to their shepherd, to whom they looked for
security, that they were waiting for his next command. In
strong contrast to the whiteness of the sheep, the dark goats
stood placidly nearby. They, too, were herded together, their
glossy dark brown hair shining in the light of the sun. While we
looked on, we were entertained by the spectacle of an Arab
farmer engaged in selling a kid. It was a most attractive little
animal, with appealing eyes which ought to have moved the
heart of the most seasoned purchaser. Since we were

unseasoned observers, we were given an unexpected shock when the seller grasped the silky-coated kid by the ear and lifted it clean off the ground, holding it up for display. To our amazement, the little animal neither showed sign of pain nor offered any form of protest. A nearby member of our party, himself a farmer, made a remark as he sensed our reaction. 'Apparently the breed has ears for lifting purposes, like our rabbits at home!' Well, there might be some comfort in the thought, but one can still feel uncomfortable at the idea. The ears seemed so slender against the animal's full weight.

We proceeded towards the other animals for which the Arab world is famous: picturesque, lithe, and so healthy, the ponies and horses were captivating. 'It is a pity we can't slip one into the plane when we are going home,' said one enthusiastic admirer with a smile. Standing placidly, these animals were enjoying all the attention lavished upon them by observers and dealers alike. The inevitable donkeys and mules, which hold such a key role in the day-to-day work of the Holy Land, stood about passively in groups of two or three. Through the higgledy-piggledy groupings of the animals, the people ambled, creating as they did so a cacophony of human voices and sounds in differing dialects and even languages. Through the noise could be heard the distinctive jangle of the tea and water seller, who carried his containers and cups like a rucksack, and by adept twisting and turning, succeeded in pouring and distributing whatever was fancied.

There were those who were in no hurry to sell, or else had already sold sufficient to justify coming to market, for they were sitting on the dry, stony ground enjoying their chat, as farmers do in every part of the world. For us there was something romantic about strolling around the market place under the ancient walls of this old city, looking at so much that had not changed since Bible times and rubbing shoulders with people from the valleys and hills who in appearance had not altered in a thousand years.

But we must move on! Nazareth, Galilee and the north were waiting. It was from Nazareth that we were to explore Lower and Upper Galilee, and visit the sites carrying the magic names associated with our Lord's ministry. To reach Nazareth, Capernaum, Bethsaida and the other sacred places clustered round the Lake of Galilee, we must needs go through Samaria.

We gathered our belongings, saw them safely stored in the

bus, said farewell to the friends we had made in the Arab hotel and thanked David, our Arab guide, for the responsible and cheerful way he had looked after our interests. He then handed us over to an Israeli guide named Naomi, who was to be our shepherdess through those parts of the Holy Land associated with the Good Shepherd. Any regrets we might have had in leaving the hotel which had been our home for the first exciting phase of our holiday, was countered by our eager anticipation of seeing Galilee.

The bus moved off and we proceeded north over the slopes of Mount Scopus. Looking backwards from this hill one has as fine a panoramic view of Jerusalem as is to be found anywhere in the area. Naomi pointed out with marked enthusiasm the university, speaking eagerly of its growth and the number of students who flocked to it from all over the world. For them the quest for academic qualification would be enhanced by the opportunity of studying in this corner of the earth, which lies at the heart of three great continents, and is so steeped in history. They would be involved with many nationalities and languages.

As the bus continued on its northerly course, we found ourselves travelling through country offering a blend of the ancient and modern. History and current affairs walked side by side. There was Samuel's tomb on the crest of a hill, and by the side of the road were standing expensive, modern villas in a wealthy suburb of Jerusalem, owned by rich Arabs. Here, King Hussein of Jordan had lived for a time. At one point we passed through part of the Jordanian territory and noticed that the number plates on Arab-registered cars were blue, and those on Israeli vehicles yellow. Here the wealthy from Saudi Arabia had their summer residences, and to facilitate speedy transport, they had laid their own private airstrip. In contrast to the modern, we passed the junction of a branch road, the road to Emmaeus, where Jesus had made the hearts of two disconsolate disciples burn within them, while He opened to them the Scriptures.

At a distance of about eight miles from the city stands the hamlet of Ramallah. Here was the resting place, a Sabbath day's journey, where Joseph and Mary once settled down for the night on their way home from Jerusalem. They had supposed Jesus to be in their company, but when they sought for Him he was nowhere to be seen. Since He was only twelve

years of age at the time, they were naturally concerned lest
something had happened to Him. Enquiries among their
kinsfolk and acquaintances yielded no comfort. Jesus was lost
as far as they were concerned. Concluding in the end that He
had been left behind in Jerusalem, they decided to make their
way back to the city. To their relief they discovered Him in the
temple, and to their amazement He was engrossed in asking
questions of the teachers. Both the teachers and the parents
were astonished at the earnestness and intelligence of this
young boy. We can imagine that Joseph and Mary, proceeding
on their way to Nazareth, had much food for thought as they
considered Jesus' words: 'What made you search? Did you not
know that I was bound to be in my Father's House?'

On a hill to the right is Bethel, associated with Jacob's
dream, but our guide drew our attention to a tradition that the
famous stone of Scone, which now rests under the Coronation
chair in Westminster Abbey, was originally brought from
Bethel to Scotland. From there it was taken to England in
Edward I's reign.

As we journeyed on we noticed that the colour of the soil
changed from a sandy to a reddish hue. We became almost as
soil-conscious as the Israeli themselves, whose worthy
ambition is to make the desert blossom as the rose. Concerned
about erosion, they have taken practical steps to counter this
danger by planting olive trees in profusion. Along with the
olive groves, forests of pine trees are being created. We noticed
Moslem villages with their houses painted in blue and green,
allegedly to ward off the evil eye. The hills are terraced, and
again planted with olive, which is now regarded as almost
sacred. We were amused to hear our guide refer to a village with
an English name, St Giles, which dates back to the days of the
Crusaders, some of whom married the natives, and made their
homes in the area.

Still travelling north, we passed Shiloh, a site associated with
those adventurous times when Israel had completed the
invasions of the Promised Land. Shiloh was the place where
the Israelites assembled together and erected their Tent of
Meeting. In time, they built a separate sanctuary which
attracted religious festivals and pilgrimages. It became the
temple for which Eli was responsible, and in which Samuel
spent his early life. Alas, the glory departed and this temple
was destroyed. Eli's sons proved irresponsible, and the people

turned away from their faith, allowing themselves to be
influenced by the pagan life of the inhabitants among whom
they had come to dwell. The Ark of the Covenant was captured
from them, most likely by the Philistines, and it never returned
to Shiloh. The site as a sacred place was subsequently
abandoned, and degenerated into ruin and desolation. The land
was occupied by Philistine garrisons and Israel found herself
under the pressure of a foreign yoke. Shiloh became an example
of the desolations which follow in the wake of faithlessness and
irresponsible living, of the effects of neglecting or abusing
God-given privileges and blessings. To this example the
prophet Jeremiah pointed, when he said: 'But go ye now unto
my place which was in Shiloh, where I set my name at the first,
and see what I did to it for the wickedness of my people Israel'.

As we proceed on our journey from Shiloh, we leave behind
the hills of Judaea and, turning a little to the west, descend into
the valley of Libonah and so enter the dividing line between
Judaea and Samaria. We were intrigued to notice the women
working in the fields, which is the general custom in the Arab
community. The men consider that their duty is to construct
and repair the buildings, and deal in the market places. We
recalled a joking remark our Arab guide had made earlier with
refence to this situation. 'A great country for men to live in!' -
evoking the acclamation of the male element of our party and
the derision of the female. He admitted that the men did quite a
bit of sitting around. A Moslem can have up to four wives, and
if he takes the notion, he can divorce any one of them quite
easily. When a woman slows up with the passing years, the
temptation is strong to bring in a younger one. A commercial
aspect is also involved, since men may trade wives for camels
and goats. The women thus provide an acceptable work force
and families have laboured for generations on the land in this
way. Now, however, the position is slowly changing. Young
people tend to leave the land and move into the towns where
they can get a good job and more attractive conditions. They
enjoy a new-found independence.

We moved northward over the plain towards an ancient
town, called by various names over the centuries with the
changing pattern of history: Shechem, Sychar, Neapolis or
Nablus. The name Schechem brings to mind the ancient town
which lies in a narrow defile between two impressive
mountains named Gerizim and Ebal. On these opposing

heights were recited the blessings and curses attending either the keeping or neglecting of the law, on the occasion when Joshua led his army to the conquest of the land of Canaan. The Israelites took their stand in the valley between the two mountains. Half of them faced Gerizim, the mount of blessing, and half Ebal, the mount of cursing. This was carried out punctiliously by Joshua who 'recited the whole of the blessing and the cursing word for word, as they are written in the book of the law.' Taking into consideration the excitement attending the event, the favourable accoustics afforded by the mountains and the still air, the imagination can catch the sense of drama. Just as the Jews revere Zion, so the Samaritans regard Gerizim as the holy mountain. At the base of these two imposing mountains lies Nablus.

The ancient name of Schechem is associated with Jacob. Schechem was one of the cities of refuge. It was under a great oak here that Jacob hid his Teraphim (the symbols of his faith), and it was here that Joshua gave his parting address to the elders.

When we think of the town of Nablus, we conjure up in our minds the circumstances that led to an unfortunate breach, that 'the Jews have no dealings with the Samaritans'. The antipathy dates back to the disintegration of the divided kingdoms of Israel (the northern) and Judah (the southern). The Assyrians defeated Israel, took captive the northern tribes and deported them, while the Babylonians destroyed Jerusalem in 586 B.C., leading Judah into captivity.

Then again we might refer to the town as Neapolis, a reminder of the Roman influence in the Holy Land. As commander of a formidable and highly trained army, Vespasian conquered the town, before being proclaimed emperor. It was left to his son Titus to complete the campaign by destroying Jerusalem in 70. The name Neapolis was imposed on Schechem, but the softening effect of Arabic changed it to Nablus. Apart from the minorities of Samaritans and Christians, the 22,000 inhabitants are Moslem. We may think of the town as Shechem, Sychar, Neapolis, or Nablus, but for Christians it is the geographical setting for that thought-provoking incident, our Lord's conversation with the woman of Samaria at the well. For Jacob's well was there and is there still. It would be appropriate to look at the well through the next window.

19. AND THE WELL IS DEEP

The modern atlas shows Sychar as a small village to the east of Neapolis or Shechem, roughly one and a half miles away from the higher centre, but near enough to warrant the old controversy as to whether Sychar was the same as Shechem. Taking into consideration the site of Jacob's well, we are given the clear impression that Sychar is a satellite village to Nablus. So in reality, it is better to think of Shechem, Neapolis and Nablus as being one and the same place, and Sychar as a hanger-on, not quite, but very nearly a suburb.

In our Lord's time this was Samaritan country, but there are scarcely five hundred Samaritans to be found there today. They are struggling desperately to survive as a race, but, with so much in-breeding caused by their deeply rooted suspicion of mixed marriages, it tends to be a losing battle. The Samaritans still limit their Scriptures to the first five books of the Bible; they still sacrifice a Passover lamb and endeavour to preserve in detail the Mosaic rites and practices, but in numbers they are dwindling.

The bitterness which existed between Jew and Samaritan has its roots in history. The Jew could not forget that when Sargon, king of Assyria, in the eighth century B.C., captured the town of Samaria, he placed the city under Assyrian governors and established a community practising a form of the Hebrew faith, which they grafted on to their own beliefs and practices. The motive was to please the god of the land. When the Hebrews flocked back to their homeland after the exile in the times of Ezra and Nehemiah, the Samaritans were strongly opposed to the rebuilding of the temple at Jerusalem, which was a burning aspiration in every Hebrew heart. Adding insult to injury, the Samaritans lent their support to Alexander, and in return, gained permission to build a rival temple on Mount Gerizim, where they sacrificed after the Jewish manner. The idea of heathen blood performing Jewish rites was anathema to the orthodox Jew, and so communication between the two races became non-existent. The Jews had no dealings with the Samaritans. The latter still worship in a modern temple near Nablus and the ruins of their ancient temple on the

top of Mount Gerizim remind us that for centuries the
Samaritans have performed the ritual of the Passover in its
entirety.

We set out for Jacob's Well, which is but a short distance from
the village of Sychar. By the side of the road is the shell of what
was meant to be a Greek Orthodox Church. At first glance one
might think that it was a substantial ruin, but a second glance
reveals it as a Church that was never completed, and while the
edifice looks sound enough at present it will eventually collapse
if nothing is done to protect the remains. One enters a doorway
where there is no door. On either side, Corinthian pillars
support a simple and attractive arch, and the eye is caught by
the mathematical beauty of stone columns jutting out from the
walls of the nave. The Church has no roof, but the walls stand
steadfast, calling out for someone to come along and finish the
job. A square stone slab, resting on a pedestal in what would be
the chancel, looks as if it had been intended for a communion
table.

The eye is then drawn upwards towards a narrow Gothic
recess in the wall in which there is a cross. Now this cross is
different. It is not made of gold or silver, wood or stone. In fact
it is an open cross built, or cut, as it were, into and through the
wall. It is located where a stained glass window is often found
in churches at home, but the attraction in this church is that no
window is in the space. It all seems so natural. The fact that
there is no roof on top of the walls means that there is nothing
to stop the showers of the rainy season from pouring in on the
thirsty ground. No doubt those who have sermons and
addresses to deliver regularly, will find some significance in the
roofless church. No man-made barrier has been erected to
interrupt the showers of blessing. Be that as it may, our
footsteps were drawn towards two small huts, one on the left of
the centre and the other on the right. Peering through the open
door of one we could see a descending stairway of stone leading
down to what would be called the crypt — in this case a
spacious room with the stone surrounds of Jacob's well
standing in ancient simplicity in the middle. Jacob's Well!
Since wells do not rove about, we know that this is an authentic
site which time has preserved for us. Before going to lean over
the low well surrounds to gaze into the depths, four Biblical
names leapt into my mind. Abraham, Jacob and Joshua, in
their time, had passed this way, and it was here that Jesus sat

by the well in conversation with the woman of Samaria.

Every pilgrim or tourist visiting the sacred sites of the Holy Land will be familiar with St. John's account of the incident of Jesus and the Samaritan woman. Accordingly it would be presumptuous to relate the story in detail, but it would do no harm to offer the impressions which certain details in the narrative throw into relief when one stands on the very spot.

It is the detailed account which St. John has given to us that heightens the vitality of the story. Travelling from Judaea, our Lord had reached Sychar, 'near to the parcel of ground that Jacob gave to his son Joseph. Now Jacob's well was there.' So the location is clearly pinpointed. The picture which comes to one's mind is that of our Lord sitting at the well, feeling weary after his journey, and resting while waiting for His disciples. The first thought which came to me at the approach to the well was its location in relation to Sychar the village. One could easily imagine Jesus choosing to sit down at this historic spot, stimulated, no doubt by its significance in the history of His people. The text tells us — 'For His disciples were gone away unto the city to buy meat.' From where Jesus sat, He would have watched them going down the rough road to the village which was not far off, to buy supplies. There is nothing outstanding in the event, but the detail is so natural that it provides a vivid and convincing account of what took place, forming the setting for the conversation which Jesus held with the woman of Samaria. The opening sentence, arising out of the natural circumstances, is very plain when one is on the spot, because the heat arouses thirst, and the well is the answer. So Jesus said to the woman: 'Give me a drink.' The woman was surprised that Jesus had spoken to her, for she recognised Him for a Jew and was not expecting Him to show her the slightest regard, since she was a Samaritan. Without going into the detail of the conversation which developed at this point, one may notice another natural remark — 'Sir, thou hast nothing to draw with, and the well is deep.' No bucket and no rope!

We were more fortunate, because, for the convenience of visitors to the well, a winch has been supplied whereby a bucket may be lowered easily into the water and subsequently raised. We all wished to have a drink from Jacob's Well, not only because of historic association, but also on account of our thirst produced by the heat. Since there was a party of us at the well, everyone looked round for someone to work the winch and do the necessary. It was one of those times when it does not pay to look strong and muscular. Without any discussion or formal vote, all eyes concentrated on a suitable candidate and general consent laid the responsible burden on the broad shoulders of a young man who was always popular with us, and even more popular then. True to his cheerful and generous disposition, he accepted the challenge and lowered the bucket. When he had satisfied himself that it was truly in the water, he began turning the winch to return it to the surface. Those near to the well were looking over the low wall with curiosity and anticipation. The vision was limited, however, because the narrow part of the structure at the top widened out very soon into utter darkness, and for a time silence descended upon us as we listened to the characteristic sounds of the winch itself on its return journey. Our friend worked on steadily till everyone felt the bucket must surely be near the top. Still he turned and turned the handle and still the bucket eluded us. The effect of sustained expectation, with no sign of fulfilment, was a flow of comment and encouragement from all gathered round. The 'wincher' in fact did not need the free advice because he himself was showing signs of frustration, which prompted him to make a final effort, thinking that the bucket must surely be near the top. Then it happened! The bucket came up with a rush, splashing some of its contents liberally over those spectators standing too close to the scene of action. There was a great scattering, accompanied by appropriate howls.

The length of time the operation had taken posed the natural question, how deep is the well? The answer that eventually emerged was that it was seventy or eighty feet! Our gallant young man was satisfied that the depth must be all of that. The well was deep indeed.

One tries to imagine the scene when Jesus sat by the well. Since there was no winch, it must have been a considerable task to haul the water to the well's mouth. There would be need for many pauses, and it is probable that much of the subsequent conversation took place while the woman rested for fresh energy. As the woman continued the conversation, she referred to another aspect of this historic place, which cannot fail to impress anyone who has the opportunity of looking down into the well: 'Art thou greater than our father Jacob, which gave us the well, and drank thereof himself, and his children and his cattle?'

It is awe-inspiring to consider how old this well is. The wells were so necessary to life in the ancient world that from generation to generation they were known and respected. Thumbing through the book of Genesis, we read of Abraham digging a well at Beershebah and calling upon Abimelech to witness that it was his, and in the next generation his son Isaac dwelt by the well Lahairoi, for where the water is, man and beast have to live. In Genesis chapter 29 we read of Jacob coming unto 'the land of the people of the east', looking for a well. He found one in a field and 'there were three flocks of sheep lying by it; for out of the well they watered their flocks.' So wherever the wells were, the nomad shepherds and their flocks gathered. The reference here is not to Jacob's well, and indeed, the Old Testament narratives do not pinpoint any particular place as Jacob's well in the sense in which the Samaritan woman refers to the well at Sychar. Here, at least, the Jew and the Samaritan agree in their tradition when they say that Jacob in his journeying stopped here and drank, watering his flocks and herds. There is no reason to doubt the tradition, and we recognise that the wells of ancient times were known from generation to generation. Like the 'everlasting hills' they were stable.

Standing by Jacob's well, we visualise the scenes of Genesis, with the nomadic tribes and individuals roving over the face of the land from well to well. Above all, we bear in mind that our Lord must have drunk from the well Himself. The narrative in St. John's account does not record the woman actually offering the desired drink, but considering the friendly approach of our Lord and the developing conversation, we may accept that, while all this was taking place, she graciously offered the water which Jesus no doubt accepted appreciatively.

Another realistic feature presents itself as we think of the event. 'The woman saith unto Him, Sir, I perceive that thou art a prophet. Our fathers worshipped in this mountain; and ye say, that in Jerusalem is the place where men ought to worship.'

One can see her make a gesture with her hand as she spoke, drawing attention to the nearby Mount Gerizim, as sacred to the Samaritans as the temple and Mount Moriah are to the Jews. It would have been unfortunate for the rest of us if the avenues of worship were limited to the sacred locations deemed paramount to man in his commendable devotion, but the Son of

Man and the Son of God came to the rescue: 'The hour cometh, and now is, when the true worshippers shall worship the Father in spirit and in truth: for the Father seeketh such to worship Him.'

There is food for much more thought in the incident, but enough has been considered to illustrate how authentic the acccount is. Standing by the well and reading the Gospel, one recognises the unmistakable stamp of truth in the recounting of an event in which one feels oneself to be almost a witness.

AT THE GOOD SAMARITAN INN

20. SEBASTE

About six miles to the north-west of Sychar is the town of
Sebaste, which was once called Samaria. It was built by Herod
the Great on the ruins of the old capital city of the kingdom of
Israel as distinct from Judah. He named it Sebaste in honour of
his patron, the Emperor Caesar Augustus, Sebaste being a
Greek form of the emperor's name. From Nablus one follows the
valley for some distance, and then the road rises steeply up the
shoulder of the mountain to a crest from which one sees an
impressive panorama of the hills of Samaria. Terraced round
this vantage point lie the fascinating ruins of a city, which in
Herod's time must have been a worthy bit of Rome in a foreign
land, and an outpost in which the Roman could taste some
flavour of home. As we move in and out of this remarkable
complex of bygone days, three lines of associated thought
present themselves.

The first is obvious on arrival. If those Corinthian columns,
lying in rows on the ground where they fell, could be set up
again with the help of some stonework, it would be possible to
walk through the forum, to take a seat in the open-air theatre
and recapture the stimulus of a Roman market. In its day,
Sebaste must have been a magnificent replica of many a
Roman city. As an architect, Herod had not spared himself or
his resources in paying tribute in stone to Caesar Augustus.
The temples, theatres, columned streets, the gates, the baths
and the forum must have made the mercenaries stationed there
feel very much part of the empire. Sitting on one of the
stone-work tiered seats, it was easy to conjure up in
imagination those people in Roman costume, occupying the
other seats round about, though they are separated from us by
over two thousand years.

Much excavation work has been taking place, guided by the
fine row of pillars, still standing in their original places like so
many ancient sentinels watching over the ruins and
supervising the renovations. Behind these columns are walls of
previous buildings at various stages of disintegration, and, as a

background to the whole scene, stands a belt of tall and flourishing trees, whose olive green colour blends handsomely with the white and grey stoneworks that are Sebaste.

As we move along the plateau containing so many well preserved walls, we come to the end of the city which commands an extensive view of the hills of Samaria. In this area the belt of trees, in varying shades of green, spread right over the tops of the hills, giving the impression that they overflow from valleys not big enough to contain them.

A second line of thought is prompted by a look over the edge of the plateau on which Sebaste stands, revealing a deep and dangerous descent into the immediate valley below. The slope is covered with debris which dates back to the destruction of Samaria in the days of King Omri. One would think that the whole Samaritan capital had been swept aside to form a level site for Herod's ambitions. Parts of the city of Samaria might possibly be excavated, but not many. Looking down upon the rubble one is reminded of an ancient prophecy of such destruction. It has truly been fulfilled.

During a very unsettled period of the Northern Kingdom of Israel, Omri put an end to the ambitions of Zimri, an officer in the army, to take over the kingship, and he similarly crushed another pretender to the throne named Tibni. Accordingly, Omri was encouraged by his soldiers to accept the throne (if encouragement he needed) and he found himself hailed as king. As it turned out, his accession proved beneficial to Israel, for he brought stability to the northern kingdom. The new king cast his eye over the flat-topped hill. It commanded a wide prospect toward the west and could be defended easily on all sides. Noting the rich fertility of the land, he chose to build the town of Samaria as his capital and the seat of government. The plain of Sharon was not far away, and he would be within easy reach of the sea, and strategically placed for support from Phoenicia, when hard pressed by the Assyrians. His career proved successful, and the 'Moabite Stone' testifies to his abilities as a warrior, since it records that the Moabites paid tribute to Israel over a period of forty years. His influence must have been considerable, because his name appears on Assyrian inscriptions with reference to 'the land of the house of Omri'. He is regarded as the founder of a dynasty in the history of the northern kingdom.

Omri bought the hill for his city from Shemer for two talents

of silver and named the town Samaria, after Shemer. This
name was in keeping with its function for it means 'watch
tower' and in time it was further fortified by the establishment
of military strongpoints scattered round the area, and
successfully survived two severe sieges by the Syrians. In spite
of auspicious beginnings, however, Omri did not remain
consistent in either character or leadership. We read in I Kings,
'But Omri wrought evil in the eyes of the Lord— For he walked
in all the way of Jereboam the son of Nebat, and in his sin
wherewith he made Israel to sin.' The direction in which
Samaria and the northern kingdom were moving is indicated in
that when Omri 'slept with his fathers' and was buried in
Samaria, the throne slipped into the hands of Ahab, his weak
son, and through marriage to the influence of the infamous
Jezebel.

So Samaria, which was built with high hopes and rich
promise, ended in ruins. The rubble spilled down the hillside
from the plateau, and Sebaste was subsequently erected in its
place. The voice of prophecy, heard in the book of Micah,
declares: 'I will make Samaria as a heap of the field, and as
plantings of a vineyard; and I will pour down the stones thereof
into the valley, and I will discover the foundations thereof ...
Samaria shall become desolate; for she hath rebelled against
her God.' Standing on top of the hill, one is not only conscious
of the desolation of Herod's ambition, but, as one looks down on
the mounds of stone of former Samaria spilled into the valley, it
would be difficult to discover a more exact fulfilment of
prophecy. Since then many excavations have taken place, and
among the more exciting finds are ivory carvings in Phoenician
style, indicative of the decorations of the 'ivory house' of Ahab,
mentioned in Kings:- 'Now the rest of the acts of Ahab, and all
that he did, and the ivory house that he made, and all the cities
that he built, are they not written in the book of the chronicles
of the kings of Israel?'

The city could boast of a bishopric in the early fourth century,
and also a cathedral when Christianity was legalised. A
smaller church was also constructed to witness to the belief that
John the Baptist had been buried there. This is the third line of
thought when one visits Sebaste — the association with John
the Baptist. The ruins of the little church stand to
approximately the roof level of what the structure once was.
Just in front of the entrance to the vestibule is a blue notice

board with the words 'Church of St John the Baptist' in
Hebrew, Arabic and English. It was built by the Crusaders,
who did so much to preserve the sites of the Holy land. The
structure of the building is composed of massive stones which
are likely to endure for ages. It is a little church which will
always conjure up thoughts of Herod, Herodias and Salome
(who danced to please the king and asked as her reward the
head of John the Baptist). There is nothing in the New
Testament narrative to pinpoint the spot where the feast took
place, but there is a verse in St Mark — 'And when a
convenient time was come, that Herod on his birthday, made a
supper to his lords, high captains and chiefs of Galilee.' Galilee
was not far away from Sebaste, although the Roman city of
Tiberias was on the lakeside itself. On the other hand, we read
that the disciples of Jesus came and took up John's corpse, and
laid it in a tomb. Was the tomb close by? Was it in Sebaste? Was
it in the region of this little church?

We stood within the ruined walls and meditated upon the
events of almost two thousand years ago, and then retraced our
footsteps observing some of the humble dwellings of local
inhabitants and contrasting them with the magnificence of
what was once Sebaste and Samaria — a royal capital, a
Roman city, complete with palaces, temples, baths, theatres,
market places, columned streets and impressive gates, not to
mention a liberal supply of mercenary soldiers! It was a step
into realism when we entered a modern shop on the edge of the
forum, to rejoice in a grapefruit drink and examine the goods
set out for sale. The time had come to move on.

As we moved north, we passed several strategically placed
police stations, and our guide explained the method whereby
the British handled law and order, when, in 1918 they were
given the mandate to govern Palestine. Their presence in the
towns was discreet, but in an inconspicuous way they
controlled the roads which were the arteries of communication.
Now we were on our way towards Nazareth, the place where
Jesus was reared and prepared for the unique life and work that
was to be specially His. As Bethlehem is associated with His
birth, so Nazareth is related to His boyhood, youth and early
manhood. We were delighted to learn that Nazareth was to be
the base from which we were to visit the Lake of Galilee, the
coast to the west and as far north as the foothills leading to
Mount Hermon. So we proceeded with excited anticipation.

When we had travelled about twelve miles north of Shechem (Nablus), and just before descending into the plain of Jezreel, our attention was drawn by our guide to a deep valley among the hills. This was Dothan, and our thoughts turned towards an event of ancient times which changed the life of Jacob and led to deep thoughts of God. His name was eventually changed to Israel. Jacob had flocks in Shechem, and he sent his older sons to feed them and look after their welfare. Evidently, in an age when communication was slow, he was concerned to know if all was well not only with the flocks but also with his sons. So he sent one of the younger sons, Joseph, to see how everything was. This is not the place to go into the whole well-known story, but Joseph did not find his brothers at Shechem and was directed by a local inhabitant to go to Dothan and he would find them there. When his brothers saw him coming they decided to take him into captivity and to put him to death. However Judah spoke on his behalf and privately engineered his release. They sold him to Midianite merchantmen who happened to be passing that way and he ended up in Egypt. This they did in revenge for his dreams.

It is the end of the story that is most relevant. As time passed, the tables were turned and Joseph then had his jealous brothers within his grasp to do as he would with them. They expected and feared he would take revenge on them, but on the contrary, he forgave them: 'I am Joseph your brother, whom ye sold into Egypt. Now therefore be not grieved, nor angry with yourselves, that ye sold me hither; for God did send me before you to preserve life.... But as for you, ye thought evil against me; but God meant it unto good, to bring to pass, as it is this day, to save much people alive.'

This spirit of grace, forgiveness and reconciliation has always been in the heart of God, and is commended to those who would live for Him and serve Him. It was reaffirmed from our Lord's Cross at Calvary, where He prayed for those who were crucifying Him — 'Father, forgive them; for they know not what they do.'

It was at Dothan, too, that the incident took place which is recorded in II Kings, vi. The king of Aram (Syria) was making war on Israel, but his efforts proved abortive and frustrating, because Israel seemed to be warned in advance of every move. The king was so concerned, that he suspected a spy or a traitor in their midst. Summoning his staff, he said to them, 'Tell me, one of you, who has betrayed us to the king of Israel?' The response was that none had betrayed him, but 'Elisha, the prophet of Israel, tells the king of Israel the very words you speak in your bedchamber.' So the king sent a strong force of chariots and horses to surround Dothan by night. In the morning, Elisha the prophet saw that he was surrounded and in despair his servant said:— 'Alas, my master! how shall we do?' Elisha prayed that the young man's eyes might be opened, and when they were, he could see that 'the mountain was full of horses and chariots of fire round Elisha' — which was a typical and attractive way of saying that his master was under divine protection, and in touch with spiritual resources. The Lord was on his side.

In our Lord's time the Jews avoided the province of Samaria, but today that is not necessary, and by contrast one and a half million Jews are said to live there. As we proceeded our guide drew our attention to the town of Jenin, which was known as En-gannin in the days of Joshua. The name En-gannin means the fountain of the gardens, and it was by this way that Ahaziah, king of Judah, once fled when he was pursued by Jehu. The reference to the gardens was appropriate; we were just entering the great plain of Esdraelon about which both Arab and Hebrew guides speak with warmth and enthusiasm. Many of Israel's greatest victories and most disastrous defeats were staged here, but now the emphasis is not so much on the military events of the past as on the agricultural prosperity which is now manifest on every side. We could see the yield of the fertile alluvial soil, the miles and miles of land, irrigated by waters flowing from the mountains which bound the valley on three sides. It is shaped like an irregular triangle stretching from the Mediterranean to the Jordan valley, contained on the south by the hills of Samaria, and on the north by the hills of Galilee. A long ridge stretches to the sea in a south-westerly direction, coming to a halt at the steep promontory of Mount Carmel. Another mountain is noticeable to the north, standing out conspicuously, and shaped like a pyramid rounded at the top. It is Mount Tabor, and it marks the area on which our anticipation is focussed, for we are looking forward to reaching Nazareth over which Tabor stands sentinel — but more about that later! The mountains of Little Hermon and Gilboa emerge on the eastern end of the plain.

Leaving the feathery palms, the orange groves, cacti and

prickly pear, the bus speeds rhythmically on a good modern road along the famous plain. For miles there is a flat, level surface and, agriculturally speaking, the plain of Esdraelon seems to have everything. Apart from its first-class soil, the ground, being flat, is easy to cultivate with modern machinery. The industrious farmer can therefore work with satisfaction and rejoice in an abundant yield.

At the end of the First World War, the plain of Esdraelon was plagued by malaria and remained a desert until, with the establishment of the Jewish state of Israel, and the enthusiasm and energy of the new settlers, it has been successfully cultivated. It is now inhabited, with villages scattered round in profusion. The plain has sought to turn its swords into ploughshares, and one hopes that it has seen the end of military campaigns.

The evidence of history shows how slow mankind is to learn. In the plain the chariots of Egypt, Assyria and Babylon thundered in deadly conflict. Barak fought with the Canaanites. Gideon contended with the Midianites. Saul and Jonathan were slain in a struggle with the Philistines. A long tale of strife may be told, stretching from the victory of Tuthmosis III in 1479 B.C. to General Allenby's defeat of the Turks in A.D. 1918. At the western end of the plain stands the fortress of Megiddo which gives its name to the Hebrew Armageddon. The name Armageddon means the Height of Megiddo, and is associated with the reference to the last battle to be fought by the nations, mentioned in the book of Revelation, when the spirits are sent out to muster all the kingdoms of the world for the final battle — a day of lightning, thunder and violent earthquake such as has never been seen before in human history, the great city would be split into three, and the cities of the world fall in ruin. Every island would vanish and not a mountain would be seen. It is in the setting of this valley that such tensions are said to come to an inevitable conclusion. Looking at those flourishing crops, we are confronted by man's choice (if choice he has) whether to engage in revenge, aggression and terrorism, or to take the roads of the Kingdom and rule of God. It is destruction or life. Here in this plain the healthy crops, like a shop window neatly dressed, display the symbols of life.

We are now travelling through 'the seed plot of God' — the site of Jezreel — a place which once knew the 'ivory palace' of

Ahab, the temple of Astarte and the machinations of Jezebel and her pagan priests. We are on the way out of Samaria and going into the southern regions of Galilee. Nazareth is less than five or six miles distant, and the view is of corn fields and stretches of vegetation. The stately line of eucalyptus trees provides an artistic contrast which might inspire a painter to pick up his brush.

We close in on Nazareth. We pass through the town of Affuleh, once a progressive town, though since the beginning of Christian pilgrimages, Nazareth has developed to the detriment of Affuleh which seems to have become static. Nevertheless, Affuleh has its historic roots and is sometimes identified with Ophrah, where Jonah, the Abiezrite, watched his son Gideon thresh wheat by the wine-press to conceal it from the Midianites. While lamenting the state of chaos and confusion into which Israel had fallen, Gideon felt the call of God — 'Go in this night, and thou shalt save Israel from the hand of the Midianites: have not I sent thee?' So Gideon became a leader and a judge in Israel, and was so revered by the men who enlisted and fought at his side that they went into a crucial battle shouting — 'The sword of the Lord, and of Gideon.' In this battle Gideon achieved a signal victory.

21. NAZARETH

When we arrived in Nazareth, we found we were to be accommodated in an extremely modern hotel with an attractive swimming pool in the heart of colourful grounds. We were surrounded by beds of roses, fish ponds, a riot of shrubs and trees designed for shelter as well as beauty. The view of the valley below and the hills beyond it, as seen from the windows of the dining hall, and the chalets in which we found rest and privacy, enhanced a welcome haven from the heat of the sun and travelling. In our Lord's time there was a well-known saying — 'Can any good thing come out of Nazareth?' It reveals how the town was derided by its critics. However, the emergence of Jesus changed all that, and the gradual developments that have taken place ever since have produced an air of progress.

The town centre lies in a hollow from which the buildings stretch up the face of the hills in all directions. It is a busy little town with shops, bazaars, market stalls and goods for sale spread out in the open air. Nazareth does not receive as much thought and consideration as it should. Even the local inhabitants could do a useful job of tidying up here and there. Bethlehem, being the place where Jesus was born, has been exalted in hymn and poetry, but Jesus could easily have been born in Nazareth, had it not been for the decree of Augustus Caesar that a census should be taken with a view to assessing taxation. St Luke records that for this census everyone had to report to his own city. 'And Joseph also went up from Galilee, out of the city of Nazareth, into Judaea, unto the city of David, which is called Bethlehem, (because he was of the house and lineage of David)'. It was while he was there that his wife, Mary, gave birth to the baby Jesus. If it had not been for the decree, we might have been singing 'O little town of Nazareth' instead of 'O little town of Bethlehem.' On the other hand St Matthew held that events never take place by chance, so it was God's intention that for His own inscrutable reasons, Jesus should be born in Bethlehem. He introduces the incident of the wise men who came to Jerusalem, asking — 'Where is He that is born King of the Jews?' Herod, the king, asked the chief priests and scribes the same question. Both were given the same answer — 'In Bethlehem of Judaea; for thus it is written by the prophet, 'And thou Bethlehem, in the land of Juda, art not the least among the princes of Juda: for out of thee shall come a Governor, that shall rule my people Israel'. Man proposes, God disposes.

Herod's sinister enquiries came to nothing, and receiving a warning, Joseph and Mary took the young child, and fled to Egypt before Herod could lay his murderous hands on the boy he feared was born to be king. The death of Herod opened the way for Joseph and Mary to return to Israel. To go to Nazareth rather than Bethlehem was again dictated by events.

When Herod died all Israel was divided into three parts: the Judaean area, or southern section, was given to the elder son Archelaus; the central section around Galilee became the territory of Antipas (the Herod of the trial and crucifixion of our Lord); and to Philip was apportioned the northern and poorest section of Batanaea, Trachonitis and the desert region of north-east Galilee. As it happened Archelaus had a cruel nature like his father, so Joseph and Mary did not go to Bethlehem but to Nazareth, their former home, since Antipas inspired more confidence. We read in St Matthew — 'But when he (Joseph) heard that Archelaus did reign in Judaea in the room of his father Herod, he was afraid to go thither, being warned of God in a dream, he turned aside into the parts of Galilee: and he came and dwelt in a city called Nazareth'.

So it was here in Nazareth that our Lord spent most of His comparatively short life on earth. Of His thirty three years He must have spent roughly twenty eight in this town, and yet, apart from the account of the journey to Jerusalem when the parents lost Him as a boy of twelve years, all that the Scriptures tell us is that 'the child grew, and waxed strong in spirit, filled with wisdom: and the grace of God was upon Him.... He was subject unto His parents. He increased in wisdom and stature, and in favour with God and man'.

Perhaps the silence on these years is not unexpected, since, for our Lord, they were the formative years through which He was growing into the awareness of His mission in the world. The part He was to take in world history was of such a nature and so unique, that it took long and thorough preparation to make the effective impact. God's work through His only Son, like all God's work, demanded infinite attention to every detail of thought, word, attitude and message. Only when the fulness of the time had come could Jesus go forth into Galilee and proclaim the evangel.

Despite the silence of these years, the visitor to Nazareth must be aware continually that Jesus looked out on the surrounding hills, scanned the plain of Esdraelon, stood on the cliff edge over which the local inhabitants once attempted to cast Him down. He was to be seen playing in the streets as a child, and as He grew, mingling with the merchants, the carpenters and the farmers. In the rough and tumble of life, He was reaching forth to His destiny. The imagination can rove freely as one absorbs the atmosphere of Nazareth.

Our guide led us to the Church of the Annunciation which is a modern building — a domed basilica, built to honour the event when Mary became aware that she had been highly favoured by God, and was to be blessed among women — 'And, behold, thou shalt conceive in thy womb, and bring forth a son, and shalt call his name Jesus'. As is the usual experience, one has to go below the modern buildings to find the sacred sites of two thousand years ago, and this applies equally to Nazareth. Underneath the Church of the Annunciation there are the remains of three Churches, one on top of another, a Byzantine, a Crusader and a Franciscan. Under the Church of St Joseph is a cave, or basement, which is indicated as the house where Jesus lived with His parents. We were told that the carpenter's shop where Joseph plied his trade stood over the cave, and was part of the structure. The cave served a two-fold purpose in that it provided shelter from the heat of summer and the cold of winter. There is a large stone slab in the form of a table at which Jesus and the family once sat. Whatever natural doubts one may have, they do not prevent one imagining Jesus as a boy, and as a youth working with his father at the ploughs and yokes to which He was to refer in illustrating the Gospel in later years. In Nazareth, generations of Christians tell the story of Jesus through Churches erected to commemorate the events. As well as the Church of the Annunciation and the Church of St Joseph, there is also the Church of Jesus the Adolescent, which is cared for by French Silesian monks. There is also a Greek synagogue, which is said to be built on the site of the Synagogue where Jesus declared His identity when reading from the Scriptures to the assembled congregation, and was subsequently rejected. He read from the prophecy of Isaiah 'The Spirit of the Lord is upon me, because he hath anointed me to preach the Gospel to the poor; he hath sent me to heal the broken hearted, to preach deliverance to the captives, the recovery of sight to the blind, to set at liberty them that are bruised, to preach the acceptable year of the Lord'. The words which gave offence followed, when he said, 'Today is this scripture fulfilled in your ears'. Those who heard were too near to the light to be able to see.

The location of fountains and wells remains static. Like the everlasting hills, their sources lie undisturbed, and this may be said of the fountain of Mary, or the Virgin's Well. At one time it was the only source of Nazareth's water supply and one can still visualise the womenfolk of the village going regularly to fetch water for household needs. Among them would be Mary, and it is only natural that in time her name should be given to the well. The stream of water emerges from the depths of a hill, and it is clean and pure.

With our minds full of the thoughts and events of old Nazareth, we walked along one of the main thoroughfares to absorb the atmosphere of the modern town. The shops which line the streets are a mingling of modern and traditional. The market area follows the usual pattern of the eastern market, with stalls set up according to the space available, and goods of infinite variety spread over and round them. Even in the main thoroughfare the merchandise bulges out on to the pavements, and likely customers have every opportunity of examining whatever they fancy. Because of Joseph's trade we were naturally drawn to the carpenters' shops. One at which we paused was quite open at the front and the workshop receded into the depths of the store, giving the impression of a cave. Around the sides were planks of wood of varying lengths, and smaller pieces, ready to be put to the lathe and fashioned into the object the workman had in mind. Most of the wood was olive and, being soft, was quickly and neatly turned into the desired shape. The carpenter at the lathe was working in full view of the public, who became fascinated as they watched a rough piece of wood, in a very short time, turned into an object of art or something of a very practical nature for day-to-day use. At the time, we paused to see what he was producing, and it turned out to be a pair of herons with all the attractive slenderness characteristic of that bird-neck elegantly raised and beak pointing towards the sky. As soon as we saw the finished article, we indicated to this artist in woodwork our

desire to buy the pair. He explained that he had yet to varnish
them and seemed amused when we preferred to take them as
they were, in their unpolished state, for we liked the appearance
of the natural wood. Seasoned craftsman as he was, it was
amazing how quickly and with what skill he could fashion a
wide variety of ornaments.

With our minds on the scriptural events of Nazareth, we
looked round for, and had no difficulty in finding, what is
known as the Mount of Precipitation. As the name itself
suggests, the reference is to the incident mentioned by St Luke,
when Jesus indicated in the local synagogue, that in Himself
the scriptural passage was now fulfilled. The local people were
outraged, not believing that the Messiah could emerge from one
of their own community. 'Is not this Joseph's son?' was the
question in their hearts and on their lips. In the face of criticism
and opposition, Jesus replied, 'No prophet is accepted in his
own country'. When Jesus pressed home His claims and
attacked their scepticism, the ruling men of the synagogue were
enraged. He was led out of Nazareth to the brow of the nearby
hill. It was their intention to cast Him down headlong, but He
escaped their clutches. The Mount of Precipitation rises with a
gradual slope, so that it is comparatively easy to reach the top,
where it comes to an abrupt end, and then the drop beyond is
sheer. On his escape, Jesus left Nazareth and made His way to
Galilee, where He entered into the fulness of His ministry.

One of the highlights of our stay in Nazareth was a visit to a
peculiarly shaped hill called Tabor. It is not difficult to identify
because of its characteristic shape, being a massive mound,
flattening out towards the top. It stands conspicuously alone on
the edge of the plain of Esdraelon.

We travelled by bus from Nazareth to the foot of the hill, and
there, at an assembly point, was a collection of cheerful taxi
drivers, standing beside spacious and powerful-looking cars,
ready to transport us to the top of the hill. They were all smiles,
as if anticipating the fun they were going to have at our
expense by the thrills of the ascent. Since the road reaches the
top of Tabor, it must needs be steep and twisting. We didn't
think of counting the number of bends at the time, but they
were numerous. Once the car was filled, the driver set off with
alacrity and without ceremony. He swerved round the curves of
the narrow road, throwing the passengers, first to one side and
then the other, in such a way that many of the womenfolk

screamed, sure that the car was going to run off the road at any minute, to plunge down the hillside. While this was going on, the driver was roaring with laughter, and at the same time tooting his horn at the groups of hikers who had chosen to walk rather than to use transport. The horn-tooting was his way of saying to the pedestrians that they would have been better off if they had used the taxi, as he had suggested to them. Their way was hard and laborious while his taxi would have provided a speedy journey, the thrill of a 'figure eight' in a fairground, and more excitement generally. The climbers must have realised this when they observed the hilarity on the faces of the passengers. Eventually, to the relief of those who were nervously inclined, the cars drew into a wide open space at the top of Tabor which acted as a parking ground.

Immediately in front of us was the Church of the Transfiguration, built to commemorate the incident of the Transfiguration of our Lord, recorded in all the synoptic Gospels. St Mark tells us of Jesus taking three of His disciples, Peter, James and John, into 'a high mountain apart by themselves: and He was transfigured before them.' The disciples became conscious of Elias and Moses appearing with the Master, whose raiment shone white as snow. Peter, knowing that this was a significant event, and feeling it was a memorable experience, suggested that three tabernacles should be set up - one for the Master, one for Moses, and one for Elias. These tabernacles were not erected in our Lord's time, but there now stands a threefold church containing a chapel associated with Moses, displaying in exquisite mosaic designs the receiving of the Law, the drawing of water from the rock, and the Burning Bush; another chapel in honour of Elias, the prophet, and a third featuring our Lord. While we sat for a moment's rest in some of the pews of the main nave, to assimilate the light effects from the windows and other aspects of an environment that had been prepared with considerable thought, devotion and loving care, an Italian Franciscan appeared as from nowhere, sat down at the organ and accompanying himself, sang lustily in a traditional tenor voice that was an inspiration to us all. Then, as unobtrusively as he had come, he slipped away, as if to leave the effect of the music and praise with us rather than draw any attention to himself. One felt that this was a personal, dedicated service he wished to render, and very pleasing it was indeed.

It will be taken for granted by the reader that the reason for building the Church of the Transfiguration on the top of Mount Tabor is a traditional belief that this was the 'high mountain apart', where the scriptural event took place. This presents us with what I would call the first 'double'. For centuries, Christian thinking has halted between two opinions as to where the Transfiguration took place. One theory locates it on Mount Tabor, but a second suggests that Mount Hermon, in the far north of the country, is the authentic spot. The latter opinion likes to associate the experience of the Transfiguration with the time Jesus took his disciples into retreat at Caesarea Philippi, and states that the place apart was in close proximity to snow-capped Hermon. Mount Hermon has also the distinction of being 'high', while Mount Tabor is not so impressive in height, rising about 1,500 feet above the plain. It is impossible to say which place should be venerated for the event, and in this double of opinion, one is thrown back on the words of our Arab guide which he used when perplexed: 'It's not where it happens but what happens that matters!'

Standing at the top of Tabor, we cannot miss the great panorama that stretches away to the hills of Samaria. We are looking at a large portion of the Plain of Esdraelon, where over twenty military campaigns were fought in historic struggles. On the western side of the mountain, we can scan the land as far as Mount Carmel on the Mediterranean coast where Elijah confounded the prophets of Baal. From Mount Carmel the plain runs inland to the Jordan Valley and is bounded on the north by the hills of Galilee, and on the south by those of Samaria. The mountains of Gilboa and Little Hermon rise out of the plain itself on the eastern side. At the foot of Mount Gilboa lies the site of Jezreel (the seed plot of God), associated with the 'ivory palace' of Ahab, the temple of Astarte, where Jezebel herself employed four hundred priests. Here at Tabor, Deborah, the prophetess, and Barak ordered their small, but resolute, army to sweep down from the hills at a strategic moment during a violent storm of hail and sleet. The plan succeeded, and they defeated the king of Hazor who had for long been a menace to the Israelites. Thinking of the providential side of the victory, the Scriptures say, 'The stars in their courses fought against Sisira,' (the captain of the army of Jabin, king of Hazor).

Historically, this whole area is rich in associations with the struggles of Israel. In Gideon's time the dwellers of the plain

were continually harassed by thieving marauders who
sometimes brought their herds and flocks with them to eat up
the rich pasturage. 'Children of the east came up with their
cattle and their tents, and they came as grasshoppers for
multitude; for both they and their camels were without
number.... They destroyed the increase of the earth, till thou
come unto Gaza, and left no sustenance for Israel, neither
sheep, nor ox, nor ass.' Gideon roused and rallied a demoralised
Israel. The invaders, eager for a fight, gathered their forces and
pitched their tents in the Jezreel valley. Gideon's forces took up
positions on the mountains of Gilboa, but he reduced his army
by selecting only 300 men to carry out a ruse that succeeded in
throwing the enemy into terrified confusion, causing them to
slay their own men by mistake. Israel had conquered by their
cry: 'The sword of the Lord and of Gideon.'

It would take a lot of print to cover the events that have taken
place on and around the plain of Esdraelon. Apart from the
Scriptural references, we could also consider the thunder of the
chariots of Egypt, Assyria and Babylon.

Before going back into the cars for the no less exciting return
journey to the foot of Tabor, we take one glance at two small
towns which are visible to the naked eye. One is Endor, and the
other Nain. While the plain has witnessed many signal
victories for the Israelites, it has, nonetheless, seen disastrous
defeats. Among the latter was that of Saul by the Philistines.
Once again the Israelites had taken up their position on Gilboa,
near to the fountain of Jezreel and the Philistines were drawn
up at Shunem. When Saul saw the forces of the enemy, his heart
melted with fear. In an effort to find out his prospects, he tried
without success, all the methods he knew to discover the mind
of the Lord. As a last resort, he looked beyond the enemy's lines
to the village of Endor, where it was said a spiritual medium
could be found. Such a person was regarded as a witch, and
Saul had already decreed that any who practised witchcraft
was to be 'cut off.' However, on the night before the battle, he
decided to throw caution to the winds and, disguising himself,
he eluded the enemy and arrived at the medium's house at
Endor. Her reaction was only to be expected. Saul said, 'I pray
thee, divine unto me, by the familiar spirit, and bring me him
up, whom I shall name unto thee.' And the woman said to him,
'Behold, thou knowest what Saul hath done, how he hath cut
off those that have familiar spirits, and the wizards, out of the

land; wherefore, then, layest thou a snare for my life, to cause me to die?'

Saul, however, assured her that in this case her life would not be forfeit. The outcome of this dramatic incident was that she succeeded in confronting Saul with Samuel's spirit, which ended the interview by saying: 'The Lord is departed from thee.... The Lord hath rent the kingdom out of thine hand and given it to thy neighbour, even David.... Moreover the Lord will also deliver Israel from thee into the hand of the Philistines: and tomorrow shalt thou and thy sons be with me' (that is, in the life beyond the grave as they would die in battle). Saul, now weak with hunger, filled with fear, shattered and demoralised, collapsed. The final issue could not be altered. When he recovered sufficiently, he made his way back to his men, but when the battle was joined, the Philistines put Israel to flight, and in the pursuit it was as Samuel had said; Saul and his sons Jonathan, Abinadab and Melchishua were slain. Saul was wounded by the archers, and appealed to his armour-bearer "Draw thy sword, and thrust me through therewith; lest these uncircumcised come and thrust me through, and abuse me.' But the armour-bearer would not; for he was sore afraid. Therefore Saul took a sword and fell upon it.'

The other village one can see is not far from Endor. It is the village of Nain, which is remembered chiefly by a certain visit of our Lord when He restored to life a young man, to the delight of all the village. St Luke, in his account, tells us that when Jesus, with His disciples and a considerable number of other people, came near to the gate of the city, they met a funeral of a young man. His bereaved mother was in great distress. The words to notice in the text are 'The only son of his mother, and she was a widow. And when the Lord saw her, He had compassion on her, and said unto her, "Weep not." ' Then he gave back to the widowed mother her only son alive again. This was an unsolicited service, given out of a heart full of compassion, and it strikes confidence and hope in every needy heart, to reflect that the heart of the Father is the same as that of the Son — full of compassion, loving kindness and mercy.

22. A CLUSTER OF WINDOWS

Nazareth proved to be a happy centre for a group of pilgrims or
tourists — call them what you will. In reality we were both.
Having the tourist's appetite to see the land of Israel, we were
also pilgrims in the sense that we were ever alert to the
associations with the events of Bible times of each place we
visited. That is why various members of the party were chosen
to read the appropriate passage of the Scriptures, when we
stood on the spot where each incident took place. This made the
printed word live to us, and never again can one read the
account without visualising the whole setting vividly.

Then there were the short services organised by our leader,
who was a minister of the Church, together with the impressive
Communion Services, brief and meaningful, held in special
places like the Upper Room in Jerusalem. On Sunday mornings
we followed the example of our Lord, Who went to the place of
worship as His custom was. In our case, the service was held in
the open air among the chalets in the grounds of the hotel. The
theme on one such occasion was reflections upon the courage of
our Lord. Without the facilities of good roads and buses,
journeys for Him were more arduous and time-absorbing. In
communicating His message, He had to break through
deep-rooted ideas which had been established over hundreds of
years. In the light of His times, His views were so radical that
one can understand why it was He could save others but could
not save Himself. Even in the twentieth century, His views may
be deemed radical. As Jesus set His face steadfastly to go to
Jerusalem, the task before Him was a perplexing one. At every
turn the prospects were discouraging. This strange land, with
its strange people, presented a mysterious background from
which to win the world for the Kingdom of God. It was indeed
difficult to make an impact so great that men might be
reconciled to God, to their neighbours and themselves. It
demanded great courage and endurance to go up to Jerusalem
where He knew His enemies awaited Him. Yet this is how God

works. He places us where we are for His own inscrutable reasons. The temptation is always to think that, given a better setting and more favourable opportunities, we could be more effective. In the most difficult circumstances and environment, our Lord took the road from Nazareth to Jerusalem, and in this lies food for thought and a challenge.

Haifa, on the Mediterranean coastline, is a flourishing sea port in a most distinctive setting. To the north lies the Plain of Acco, while to the south, the Plain of Dor spreads out beyond Wadi Zerqua into the marshy Plain of Sharon. At the point where Haifa stands, the coastal plain between Acco and Dor narrows to a few hundred yards. Within this space lies the harbour area, which contains first class facilities for the shipping of the Mediterranean. This has been called the first tier of Haifa. Further up, the second tier clings to the side of the impressive limestone hill which rises to the famous Mount Carmel. This tier is the shopping area, and has the everyday atmosphere of the business and mercantile world. The third tier is the residential area, which commands a sweeping view of the town and harbour, the hills of lower Galilee beyond the Plain of Megiddo and part of the escarpment which runs from Mount Carmel to the hill country of Ephraim. This third tier is crowned by Mount Carmel itself, the scene of Elijah's contest with the prophets of Baal. Because of the exalted position of the Mount, the answering of God by fire must have been a spectacle to be observed for miles and miles, north, south, east and out at sea on the west. When all the people saw that the God of Elijah was victorious in sending fire and confounding the prophets of Baal they chanted triumphantly, 'The Lord, He is God; the Lord, He is God.' This event happened at a time when the land had not known rain for three years. We can picture the prophet standing on the top of the hill, viewing the same magnificent panorama that can be seen today, and searching the horizon across the sea for signs of a change in the weather. The threat of a water shortage was serious. Burying his face in his mantle, and breathing a prayer, he sent his servant to look out towards the sea. At last a cloud appeared which seemed no larger than a man's hand. It was the herald of rain which proved to be a welcome Godsend.

Here also, hedged in by magnificent Persian gardens, is a temple built in the style of the Parthenon. In the bright sunshine, it gleams in white and gold. This is the Bahai

Temple, the centre of a faith which seeks to assemble the best of many different religions, a synthesis. As it is in Moslem circles, the shoes must be removed before entry to indicate that inside, one stands on holy ground. The body of the Founder is said to be concealed within a beautiful casket on display in a room sealed off by a glass partition.

The name Esdraelon is but a Greek form of the Hebrew Jezreel (the seed plot of God). It was likewise called the valley of Megiddo, after the town in the vicinity around which many desperate battles were waged. Military conflicts involving names like Alexander, Pompey, Vespasian, Saladin and Napoleon took place here. Here too, the Crusaders fought. Megiddo reveals layers of geological information, stretching from 4000 B.C. to A.D. 300. Excavations have unearthed Canaanite temples, Egyptian and Hebrew seals, Solomon's 'chariot' city and an impressive wealth of ancient culture.

Further down the coast after a half hour's journey, we stopped at Caesarea. Here are the ruins of what had been a flourishing Mediterranean port in the time of our Lord. It was built at a point on the coast which offered easy contact between Rome and the outposts of that Empire. It was one of Herod's triumphs, for here he erected a town so Roman in architecture and environment, that the Roman administrators who used Caesarea as their headquarters, the Roman governors who felt it safer and wiser to be based there with their troops, the Roman citizens who were living there for various reasons — all must have felt very much at home. It was a living touch of Rome in a foreign land.

Herod undertook the building of Caesarea in honour of Caesar Augustus in 25 B.C., and it took twelve years to finish. It was a town to rank among the most up-to-date in the Roman Empire, and in conceiving the building of it and monitoring its growth, Herod not only honoured himself, but also Augustus who gave it its name. Looking at the ruins of Caesarea today, one cannot help thinking of the complex personality of Herod the Great. Endowed with a good measure of diplomatic acumen, and possessing gifts that could plan and construct a city like Caesarea, he could rise to the heights of inspiration and sink to the lowest depths of depravity and despair.

In the days of its splendour, Caesarea's impressive streets led down to a harbour which was useful and safe. This was assured by a vast mole which stretched far out to sea, and the port proved attractive to the shipping of the Mediterranean. The streets were interlaced in an attractive pattern. It was a town designed for power and magnificence. This great sea fortress could boast of an amphitheatre and all the other facilities associated with Roman life and entertainment. Little wonder Caesarea became the Roman headquarters, as it was in the time of our Lord. From here the governors went up to Jerusalem, at the Passover seasons, with regular troops at the ready should any trouble arise in that turbulent city. It was here, in A.D. 69, that Vespasian was proclaimed Emperor by the soldiers, and by A.D. 70 Caesarea was regarded as the capital of Judaea.

As we stood on the flagstones and observed the crumbled town, we felt so close to the Roman atmosphere of bygone days, that we seemed out of place, dressed as we were in our twentieth-century clothes. It is a town for the toga, the forum and the auditorium.

One of the best preserved features of Caesarea is its ancient amphitheatre with its rows upon rows of stone terraces built in a great semicircle, rising up against the skyline and looking down upon the flat, stone stage where the performers' words can be heard clearly in every direction. Standing almost a hundred yards away from the stage, a small group of us could hear quite remarkably, the voices of other members of our party engaged in conversation in the stage area. The accoustics are phenomenal, and you can imagine how delighted I was, one evening at my own home, on turning on the television, to see and hear the modern Israeli orchestra playing from that same amphitheatre. The music sounded so harmonious and true, and the performance radiated a sense of hope and achievement. One felt that modern Israel is alert to the possibilities of Caesarea, which may become alive again. What Shakespeare has put into the mouth of Mark Antony, with reference to Caesar, that the evil that men do lives after them, but the good is often interred with their bones, may be given a significant twist. In the case of Herod, we may discover an exception, since there is just that possibility that in time, with the revival of places like Caesarea, a little bit of the good he did may be resurrected and survive. It could conceivably happen that another generation may speak once again about Caesarea in the same living way as we do about Haifa and Tel Aviv. In building Caesarea, Herod secured for himself the favour of the Emperor and simultaneously his

own destiny. He succeeded in creating some prestige for the
Jewish nation, and developed among many of his people a
consciousness of the benefits Rome could offer. Yet, in spite of
all the benefits Herod bestowed, he goes down in history as an
alien, an Idumean, a friend of the hated and dominating power
of Rome, and a heathen at heart. In spite of all his efforts he
could never make Rome's presence in Judaea acceptable or
tolerable to the nation. A mutual hatred remained between
Herod and the majority of his subjects.

Before moving on from Caesarea, it is worth taking note of
the remains of an aquaduct with a tablet bearing the name of
Pontius Pilate. We are told in the Acts of the Apostles that it
was at Caesarea that Cornelius, the man who was the means of
converting Peter to the idea of accepting Gentiles into the fold,
was stationed. It was also at Caesarea that the Apostle Paul
was imprisoned under Felix, was tried by Festus and stated his
case before Agrippa II.

A MOSAIC IN THE CHURCH OF THE MULTIPLICATION

23. HIS LAKE

The time had come for our visit to the Lake of Galilee and every member of our party looked forward with natural anticipation to seeing the places where Jesus did so much of His preaching, His teaching and His healing. It was here that He called into service Simon and Andrew, while they were casting their net into the sea, and James and John who were in the ship by the side of the lake, mending their nets. It was here that Matthew used to go down to the lake and listen to Jesus expounding on the theme of the Kingdom. He was so impressed, that, when Jesus stopped at the receipt of custom where he worked and invited him to join Him, he rose up without hesitation and followed Him. He had sailed these waters, walked on these waters and preached from these waters, using a boat as His pulpit while He held the multitude spellbound. Now we were going to walk by Galilee and sail across to the other side as the Master often did. Naturally our hearts were stirred within us.

Galilee is a province of the Holy Land, which divides itself into Upper and Lower Galilee, but when we think of this magic word we have only one image, and that is the lake — His Lake. At certain points of history three different names have been applied to the lake, but the one that has emerged triumphant is Galilee. Some maps use the name Chinnereth, associated chiefly with Old Testament times, and, like all Hebrew names, it has its meaning (a harp), because of its shape. In the days of the Roman Emperor Tiberius, Herod decided to call the lake Tiberius, to honour and please the overlord whose goodwill he always sought. Yet this name did not last, because of the antipathy of the local people to their Roman rulers. The name Galilee, meaning a circle, survived and surmounted any opposition. The circle is the perfect figure, whole, symmetrical, complete, rounded off in every way, the principle on which the universe is built, where sun, moon, stars and planets move in orbit, a worthy symbol of the work of the Master Whose presence at Galilee has given the lake something akin to immortality — His Lake.

As our bus approached the crest of the hill (one of the many that surround the lake), we were governed by an irresistable excitement and an eagerness for the first glimpse. Then it came, a glittering patch of blue, standing out in the midst of the green foliage of palm and banana trees, with thickets of oleander, shrubs in profusion and golden cornfields in the foreground. In the background stood the barren grey and fawn hills around and beyond Gergesa on the far side of the water. While we coasted downhill, we appreciated the wonder of it all — to have the opportunity of walking where He walked and standing on the spot where He shared the loaves and the fishes with the multitude, of lingering for a time at Magdala, of pausing at Tabgha and Bethsaida, and finally meditating at Capernaum — His city — before moving on to where the river Jordan enters the lake, near to the spot where Jesus was baptised by John.

While descending to the town of Tiberias on the edge of the lake, the atmosphere was getting progressively warmer and warmer, and we were aware indeed of going deeper into the Jordan gorge. We were dropping to almost 700 feet below sea level. Because of the height of the hills surrounding the lake on every side, and the natural changing temperatures ranging from their summits to the surface of the waters, it is not surprising that when violent currents of air are funnelled through the hills sudden storms can lash the sea into a fury. However, all was calm for us and the sea could not have been more friendly. The lake is about thirteen miles long and seven wide, and we were anticipating a sail from Tiberias to Ein Gev on the other side. How often Jesus must have made this crossing! The thought enhanced the experience. Tiberias is a centre from which the modern tourist sets out to visit the sites where Jesus did so much of His inspiring work, and is a settlement with historic associations as well as modern appeal. It stands, therefore, for things ancient and modern.

We would have liked to spend more time in Tiberias, which has a chequered history, but our main objective was the lake. Even if we had no knowledge of the past, evidence that the influence of ancient Rome is not dead can be clearly seen. There are typical flagstones and open promenades echoing the spirit of the old Empire, and the visitor is not surprised to learn that the town, which was built around 20 B.C., was named like the lake itself by Herod Antipas in honour of Tiberius, who succeeded Augustus as emperor. The ruins of Herod's castle, a stadium and the ancient walls remain as witnesses.

Tiberias was shunned at first by the Jewish authorities, because an excavation revealed that it was built over a graveyard. It was therefore pronounced 'unclean'. The situation changed, however, in A.D. 70 when Jerusalem was razed to the ground. The Jewish leaders who had their headquarters in Jerusalem were now forced to look elsewhere for suitable accommodation. Their attention focussed on Tiberias, and since it presented all the proper facilities, it was decided to set up their headquarters there. Forgetting the former animosity, they made it an administrative centre for Rabbinical culture, and it was at Tiberias that the Mishna and Talmud were compiled. Tiberias also saw the defeat of the Crusaders by Saladin in the year 1187, but it somehow managed to survive while all the other towns dotted around the lakeside, and mentioned in the New Testament, disappeared. The places where the towns and villages once stood are marked only by a few ruins, or the bits and pieces that have been excavated. Tiberias, however, still lives, and has every appearance of surviving far into the unknown future.

In the days of our Lord it was a town which attracted many sick people suffering from varying degrees of illness. They were drawn to the Hot Springs which had a reputation of possessing healing qualities, for Tiberias was one of the spas of the middle east. Consequently when Jesus was engaged in His healing ministry, many patients sought after Him, in need of His help. The impression we have of our Lord doing His work of healing is that He was often under pressure from the many demands laid upon Him. He could scarcely find time for rest. It is very likely that many of the halt, the lame, the blind, the paralysed and the diseased were brought to Him from Tiberias, and they mingled with the many others already there. The healing ministry of our Lord must have taxed His physical, mental and spiritual powers and energy.

We made our way to the harbour and found a boat waiting and ready to put to sea. I suppose one would call it a double-decker, for one could choose to sit in the shelter of an open-sided cabin which held about twenty people, or take a position on the upper deck directly above, exposed to the sun and the open air. Either deck offered an uninterrupted view of the entire lake. Many of the party decided to sit on the upper

deck, but some opted for the cabin, reasoning that they would
be sheltered from the direct rays of the sun. It made no
difference! The air was so hot, above or below, that we might as
well have been travelling in a car with its heating on full during
a heat wave. The fact that we were ploughing over the surface
of the lake did not alter the temperature. In the prow of the boat
was a young man with swarthy skin, black hair and a beard to
match. My wife and I felt like saying 'snap' as we
simultaneously began to say that he could be Simon Peter.

The only disturbance to the mirror-like calm of the lake was
the wavelets set in motion by our boat. When we approached
the far shore and the little harbour of Ein Gev, a picture was
framed in my mind I shall never forget — a clump of trees, the
brilliant blue of water and sky, blossoming shrubs, a small jetty
with anchored boats reflected in the calm, soft waters of the
lake.

Ein Gev was like an oasis against the background of the arid
hills beyond. The general effect was a tropical profusion of
greens, browns, gold, fawns, greys and mauves, like the country
round Jericho. Ein Gev itself is an attractive little habitation
which is mainly involved in the fishing industry. Its harbour
and environs provide many captivating scenes that would
appeal to the artist. The kibbutz there is well established,
having been founded in 1923. The Festival of Music, which is
held annually during Passover Week, has proved popular.

Traditionally, it is said that it was near to this place that the
incident took place which is mentioned by St Mark in the fifth
chapter of his Gospel. Jesus had crossed the sea as we had just
done. When He left the ship He was confronted by a powerful
man who was mentally deranged. He had been 'dwelling
among the tombs; and no man could bind him, no, not with
chains'. Briefly, the man saw Jesus and approached Him in a
threatening manner, saying 'What have I to do with thee,
Jesus, thou Son of the most high God. I adjure thee by God, that
Thou torment me not.' Jesus knew that this man would need
some demonstration of his healing, so He said 'Come out of the
man, thou unclean spirit'. As the devil left the man some
nearby swine ran in panic over a steep place and down into the
sea, and the man was cured. He was then able to lead an
ordinary, normal life, to the astonishment of all who had
known him. So we were standing in 'the country of the
Gaderenes'.

We also recalled how Jesus would retreat to this side of the
lake on occasions, to find a little respite, to instruct His
disciples and to enjoy their fellowship. Soon there were many
boats following Him, and those who had no transport walked
round the lake and sought Him out.

As we were leaving Tiberias, our guide referred to the branch
of the Church of Scotland, which is doing good work through
the hospital, and to her contribution to education through the
schools in Jaffa and Jerusalem.

To the north of Tiberias are the Galilean beaches. Swimming
here was very different from the Dead Sea. The waters of the
lake were as calm as a mirror, although sudden storms can lash
them into fury. Not far away at Peniel-by-Galilee is the little
Y.M.C.A. Church, where Dr Harte lived and gave many years of
faithful and devoted service. The Harte Memorial Chapel, built
as an appreciation of his work, has a Gothic window which
offers an inspiring view of the Sea of Galilee. This thought
suggests a practical way in which we may arrange this chapter
on the Master's Lake. We may regard the sea as the main centre
piece and now take a look at the little windows round the sea.
We have already looked at Tiberias, so we go on to Magdala.

When we reached the site, our guide informed us that it was
yet to be excavated, and that is all that can be said! No village
here, no dwelling place, no industry! We must wait patiently
until the excavations are taken in hand and, no doubt, the
pilgrims of the future will gain a more impressive picture of
what Magdala once was when the foundations are revealed.
This is likely to be interesting, as we discovered when we saw
the excavated walls of Peter's house at Capernaum, which were
very different from what we had expected. So it will probably be
with Magdala. Although the village has disintegrated and
disappeared under the weight and neglect of the years, yet it
will never be forgotten. The historians keep reminding us that
the Sea of Galilee and its shores were once thriving centres
of industry and commerce — everything to do with the fishing trade flourished. Boats were built, repaired and renewed.
Fish had to be cured. Fresh water had to be laid on from
surrounding wells and springs. Magdala itself had a flourishing pottery works. The cooper's trade prospered in Capernaum
as barrels were hammered together for fish. As far as Magdala
is concerned, no one would now know that the smoke and
smells of the dyeing trade had hung over the village

there is little to show now for the industry of former years, but when the archaeologists have completed their work, no doubt the picture will be different.

A second reason why Magdala will not be forgotten lies in the references to it in the New Testament. All the evangelists tell the story of Mary Magdalene (of Magdala). She had been in great need of help, being possessed of devils, as the terminology of her times described her. Jesus set her free from her sins and obsessions, and she became a devoted follower. St Luke says she 'ministered unto him' of her her substance. We find her again standing by at Calvary, watching from a distance and feeling deeply for her Lord. Her loyalty Mary Magdalene, out of whom He had cast seven devils.' So wherever the Gospel is preached, Mary will be remembered and so will Magdala.

Further north there is a wealth of fertility by the side of the lake. Here rich oats and banana groves extend over the coastal Plain of Ginossar. The modern name does not disguise that it is the old name of the lake brought up to date. St Matthew refers to this part of the country in the passage describing Jesus and His disciples coming to land after the unnerving experience of the storm on the lake. He records 'And when they were gone over, they came into the land of Gennesaret.'

The various sites on the shore of the lake are not marked by towns like Tiberias, but as each location came to be discovered, a Church was built to mark the spot and to offer something tangible to the expectant visitor. For instance, it was not difficult to know the reference when we entered the little Church of the Multiplication of the Loaves and Fishes.

The association here of this little church is with the incident mentioned by St Luke where he tells the story of Jesus speaking to the multitude in a desert place. They were so captivated by what He was saying, and so expectant for more to follow, that they showed no sign of dispersing as the day wore on. Hungry or not, they were too fascinated to leave. Being concerned, the disciples suggested to Jesus that He should send them away to get food. Jesus replied to them 'Give ye them to eat.' The disciples protested by pointing out that the only resources available were 'five loaves and two fishes'. Without going into all the details, it is sufficient to say that Jesus used the resources and the multitude was fed. The account begins at verse ten of chapter nine which reads, 'And the apostles, when they were returned, told Him all they had done. And He took

them, and went aside, privately, into a desert place belonging to
the city called Bethsaida.'

H. V. Morton, in his book *In the Steps of the Master*, tells us
how he visited a hospice run by a Rhinelander called Father
Tapper, where he found hospitality. Father Tapper told him of
an exciting discovery in his grounds. Apparently his Arab
helper was digging in the garden, when he saw gleams of gold
and green and brown flashing up at him. Rushing into the
house he reported his find and together, with bare hands, they
gently uncovered what turned out to be the mosaic floor of an
ancient Christian church. Subsequently, they learned it was the
floor of a church erected some time in the fourth century. In
order to preserve this important find, they covered it with soil
for protection, and Father Tapper vowed that one day he would
build a church over the spot to save and guard this site. This
dream was realised, and here we were, standing at the very
place and inside the little church.

We were not allowed to walk on the original aisle, which had
been roped off for obvious reasons, but the floor was in good
order and in excellent state of repair. The mosaics witnessed to
the loving care and trouble these early Christians took to give
expression to the gracious faith which bound them together.
Against a comparatively plain background, the design
consisted of a basket holding five barley loaves, and on either
side the two small fishes. Here and there were dark green
peacocks and other birds, and the fact that the whole area was
designed in such tiny mosaic stones, reveals indeed that they
were engaged in a labour of love. Little did the congregation
know then, that their practical witness would speak to a party
of folk from the North of Ireland, seventeen centuries later. We
were looking into the roots of the Church's growth, and well
might this lovely Church, nestling on the shore of Galilee, carry
the name of the Church of the Multiplication of the Loaves and
Fishes, because millions of souls have passed through this life
and into the beyond, knowing that Christ 'is able to do
exceeding abundantly above all that we ask or think, according
to the power that worketh in us'.

Here we are aware of another double. As we recall, two places
— Mount Tabor and Mount Hermon — are claimed as the
location of the Transfiguration. Two places are also claimed as
the site where the multitude was fed. It is said that the
Bethsaida here mentioned by St Luke, was on the lake-side

between Tiberias and Capernaum. On the other hand, a different opinion maintains that the event took place on the eastern side of the river Jordan, some way upstream from Capernaum at a spot called Bethsaida Julias. While it is possible that excavation may produce some evidence that will resolve this problem, in the meantime it is very tempting to assume that the actual location is the site of the little church. St Matthew refers to 'a desert place', but it is certainly no desert place today, for, in close proximity to the Church, are fields of rich corn and other crops. The resources in terms of raw material, when turned into bread, would satisfy the hunger of thousands. Certainly, the environment around Bethsaida Julias also conforms to what we gather from the Gospel narrative. So, once again, we are forced to keep an open mind and accept for a second time the convenient dictum that it is what happens and not where it happens that is most important.

The Church of the Multiplication of the Loaves and Fishes is one of a trio of Churches which mark different incidents in the life and work of our Lord. A second sanctuary is named the Primacy of St Peter. The main interest here is an impressive rock, claimed to be the place where Jesus, after His resurrection, prepared a meal of fish and bread for His disciples. However, since our time was limited and we had other sites to visit, we did not get the opportunity to visit this church.

A third church we did visit, but when we arrived it was packed with people to full capacity and a service was in progress. It is called the Church of the Beatitudes. The building is of modern appearance, octagonal in shape and supporting an attractive dome. A colonnaded portico runs round the three sides overlooking the lake. We had the opportunity of walking round the portico and looking out across the peaceful lake, while the sound of hymn-singing emanated from the congregation within. The church is built on the edge of a ridge that reaches out to the rim of the sea, and we paused there long enough to ponder over those sayings of Jesus which this church commemorated. Whether it was the peacefulness of the lake and its tranquility, or the soothing effect of the hymn-singing lingering in the still air, or the glory of the shrubs and flowers or perhaps a combination of all three, the theme going through my mind was the phrase of the apostle Paul, 'the peace of God which passeth all understanding', and the Master's own words: 'Blessed are the peacemakers, for they shall be called the children of God.' The eight windows of the octagonal-shaped church each carried the words of one of the Beatitudes from the Sermon on the Mount.

It was now time to travel to the northern end of the lake and visit Capernaum, where our Lord spent so much of His time and did such gracious work. If the Sea of Galilee is to be called His lake it is fitting that Capernaum should be called His city. Accordingly we give it a window to itself.

FISHING IN THE LAKE OF GALILEE

24. HIS CITY

In the fourth chapter of his Gospel, St Matthew tells us that Jesus left Nazareth and came to dwell at Capernaum. An old record calls Capernaum the 'city of consolation'. It certainly proved a great consolation to our Lord, for Capernaum extended a very warm welcome to Jesus in contrast to the rejection of Nazareth. Here at the northern end of the Sea of Galilee, He was free to preach, to heal and to teach. Capernaum had never any reason to regret the coming of Jesus of Nazareth, and although the town, over the years, fell into decay, its name has lived on, and one hopes it will be resurrected in time. Even should this fail to materialise, the name of Capernaum will never die, because Jesus lived and worked there. What we see of Capernaum today, however, cannot possibly resemble the town in the time of our Lord. Then, it was a prosperous centre and a military station. What we find today, however, is sufficient to bring to life those incidents of the New Testament which capture our imagination

Two thousand years have eroded Capernaum almost out of existence. What is left consists of either excavations or resurrected ruins. Three main groupings within the town have survived:- a collection of Roman stonework and pillars, which gives the town the flavour of Roman occupation, including part of the old edifice which portrays in stone the Ark of the Covenant of Old Testament times, and which is an authentic sketch of what it looked like; a fairly well-preserved and partially reconstructed synagogue, which was also a meeting place in the town, and frequented by our Lord; and finally, the excavated outline of the walls of Peter's home which rise to about four feet in height.

The piles of stone and masonry, which have been collected together, tell us of the glory which was once Capernaum. These relics of bygone days bear the stamp of Roman design and architecture. When we bear in mind that the Jews were a nomadic race (not always by intention), and in one sense may be deemed so still, for they are scattered over the face of the earth, then we can appreciate that they had not much opportunity to develop a distinct architecture of their own. Also bearing in mind that Tiberias (a little further down the lakeside) had been built in the Roman idiom to impress the emperor, it is not difficult to discern why Capernaum showed something of the Roman influence as well.

In our Lord's time, Capernaum was one of the most flourishing towns on the lake. Ringed with eucalyptus trees and brightly coloured gardens, it possessed a sheltered bay with a natural harbour; a hive of activity for fishing boats and with the noise of coopers making the barrels, it was a centre of life and industry which provided a perfect base for our Lord's ministry. While the inhabitants learned much about building construction from the Romans, nevertheless in those things which were indigenous to their own history and traditions, they were skilled and dedicated. One stone carries a sketch of the pot of manna, while others portray the paschal lamb, the seven-branched candlestick, the star of David and the Ark of the Covenant, already mentioned. These bear the Hebrew stamp.

The second-century synagogue is one of the best preserved ancient edifices in the Holy Land. It is generally believed to have been built on the lines of the synagogue frequented by our Lord, and some would hold that it may be the one presented to Capernaum by the Roman centurion who loved the Jewish nation. We were told by our guide that it was first excavated and then renovated, and since research still goes on, it is most likely that further renovation will continue as original stonework emerges. If it is a rebuilt or renovated structure it would go back to the third century, and either way, one is standing on the sacred ground where Jesus walked and worked.

One approaches the synagogue from the left-hand side, and it stands picturesque in its simple ruin of large, fawn coloured stones. Three steps lead up to a platform of large flagstones in Roman style, which, no doubt, was the floor of a vestibule. Two further steps lead through what was once the doorway to the paved floor of the synagogue itself. At the far end of the court stand four columns in the area from which the service was conducted, and these four pillars supported the classic entableture and architrave which in their architectural simplicity remain impressive today. Beyond the columns, the back wall and the left-hand wall, rising almost to their original height, remain, and the enchanting ruin lies open to a light blue sky. The romance of the whole picture is awakened by a tree in the background, the branches of which add a pleasing contrast of colour to the pale stonework of the foreground. On this spot He taught on the Sabbath days. 'And they were astonished at His doctrine: for His word was with power.'

Fifty years ago, the visiting pilgrim would have been as curious as we to see where the big Fisherman's house once stood. It was there that Jesus took up His abode, and from there He worked. These visitors would not have been as fortunate as we were, because a great deal of excavation has taken place since then, which has revealed not only a clear outline of the foundation of the lower walls of the house, but a large plan of the rooms has been drawn and erected on a board so that the whole layout is explained. It must have been quite an extensive home, built in an octagonal shape, with joining passages, and is something quite different from anything we had visualised or expected. The view from its various rooms must have presented a regular picture gallery. To the south would have been three or four views of the Lake of Galilee; to the north the synagogue and the landscape beyond; to the east the hills above Gergesa, and to the west, shrubbery and eucalyptus trees.

While it is true that Capernaum today is silent, in contrast to the scene of noise and activity it once was, yet that silence is not the handicap one might suppose. One could linger on in the meditative atmosphere while St Matthew recalls to us the day on which our Lord called Simon and Andrew, James and John, who were fishermen, to become fishers of men; while St Mark tells of the impact of His addresses in the synagogue, 'And they were astonished at His doctrine: for He taught them as one that had authority and not as the scribes'; while St Luke records His reading from the prophet Isaiah concerning the commission of the Messiah. He describes it thus: 'The Lord hath annointed me to preach good tidings unto the meek'; and St John outlines the theme of the bread of heaven, ending with the lovely proclamation, 'I am the bread of life; He that cometh to me shall never hunger; and he that believeth on me shall never thirst.' In the quietude of Capernaum, and the tranquility of Galilee, His is the gentle voice we hear, for this is His Lake and this is His city.

To see everything one would like to see in the Holy Land would require considerable time, and since we must needs return to Jerusalem and visit the places associated with the drama that surrounded the last days of our Lord's earthly ministry, we cannot linger in Galilee beyond visiting two towns. The first is not far from the Mount of Beatitudes and is situated on the side of a hill in Upper Galilee. It is called Safed. As we journeyed towards it, we felt the bus toiling noticeably on an uphill trail. By the time we reached our destination, we had ascended 3,500 feet in 20 miles. It is indeed a city which cannot be hid.

Although Safed has historic links with the past, its reputation is mainly modern compared with most towns in Israel. It is a spot which appeals to Jewish immigrants who, because of persecution or some other reason, wish to emigrate from their country of habitation, to find a new life and a more congenial one in this land which has so much to offer them traditionally. In leaving home, they are coming home.

In the fifteenth century, several waves of Jewish immigrants settled in Safed, (such as the Sephardin), expelled from Spain in the year 1492. Many worthy, intelligent and cultured Jews from this background brought with them the qualities which have put Safed on the map. The same could be said of a later wave of immigrants, called the Ashkenazim, whose roots were found in the region of Armenia. They brought with them a religious fervour and tradition which left its mark on their new-found community. Some would claim that they are descended from one of the races mentioned in the tenth chapter of the Book of Genesis, under the heading of 'the sons of Gomer: Ashkenas, and Riphath and Togarmah.' In time this race was identified with Germany by the later Jews, so that the Ashkenazim is the name given to Polish and German Jews. These two groupings practise different rituals, and their pronunciation of the Hebrew varies, but their doctrine is the same and they mix socially and commercially.

The climate in Safed with its mountain air is so pleasant that it provides a further inducement to the many immigrants from a wide variety of lands, who seek the satisfying way of life they

anticipate in the Israel that they love. The blend of cultures
engenders enrichment for all. The United States has also
provided a goodly number of Jewish immigrants, and so Israel
now rejoices in a vast cultural blend of both European and
American. Welded together by a common faith, they are
establishing a homogeneous life.

We were greatly impressed by the Art Centre. The building
itself is artistic and pleasantly enhanced by a neat little
minaret. Before going inside, we paused to admire the exciting
designs in wrought iron, the figures in bronze and the large
sculptures in stone. Once inside, we viewed painting after
painting, depicting the impact of their history and experience
upon the artists, the appreciation of a new-found freedom
linked to a homeland of their own, and the reaching out to the
new and the modern life of Israel.

One of the intriguing features of Safed is the steepness of the
streets. The houses stretch up and down the hillside, tier above
tier, and the panoramic view is fantastic, from whichever
standpoint you may look at it. Although this town has emerged
into prominence in comparatively recent times, we bear in mind
that it was once the centre of Cabbala mysticism — a secret
system of theology and metaphysics practised among Jews,
and related to the Zohar (Book of Light and Splendour)
attributed to Shimon bar Yochai around the second century
A.D. The other revered book was the Book of Creation, ascribed
to Rabbi Akiba, who died in 135 A.D. Safed is therefore a town
of traditional Jewish learning and religion, but looks forward
into the future — Safed ancient and modern!

26. WATER INTO WINE

Doctor Leslie Weatherhead in his book *It Happened In Palestine*, reflects that if a present-day native of Cana were to enter the Abbey Church of St Peter, Westminster, on the occasion of some brilliant society wedding, he would be a little surprised to hear the name of his home town mentioned during the service. It is an even more fascinating extension to the thought, that in the smallest country church in the most isolated parts of the Christian world, the officiating minister or priest would read from the respective Book of Public Worship or Common Prayer or Order, on the occasion of the humblest wedding — 'There was a marriage in Cana of Galilee and both Jesus was called and His disciples to the marriage.' So the little village of Cana has been placed on the map, and immortalised wherever the New Testament is read.

Before we reached the town, the bus stopped at a vantage point from which we had our first glimpse of Cana, which lay round a gradual curve on the road. When we had alighted, our guide drew our attention to a particular corn field to the left of the view in front of us, but a short distance away and close to the village itself.

The corn field is associated with an incident recorded by Matthew, Mark and Luke, which has a bearing on our Lord's teaching with regard to the Sabbath. Jesus and His disciples happened to be walking along the pathway beside a field of corn. The ears of corn were ripe, and, since they were hungry, they began to pluck and eat them. Some of the Pharisees were quick to take notice, for they were ever sensitive to the prolific rules and regulations regarding the Sabbath. They took the opportunity of approaching and confronting Jesus. 'Look, your disciples are doing something which is forbidden on the Sabbath.' Jesus answered in such a way that the legalistic fault-finders were confounded: 'Have you not read what David did when he and his men were hungry? He went into the House of God and ate the consecrated loaves, though neither he nor his men had a right to eat them, but only the priests. Or have ye not read in the Law that on the Sabbath the priests in the temple break the Sabbath, and it is not held against them?'

The Master had the capacity to break through the letter to the spirit of the Law, and expose hypocrisy; to emphasise the positive approach to living in God's presence in God's world by seeking first His Kingdom, knowing that all other things would be added. He pointed to the fundamentals when He asked them to consider the text, 'I require mercy, not sacrifice.' In the light of His spirit, teaching and attitude, it is priorities which have to be considered and not even the Sabbath can deny the works of necessity and mercy. Work and worship are thrown into the scales, and neither ought to be found wanting. In probing the depths of our Lord's teaching, we sense the liberty that is always found where the Spirit of the Lord is, and the significance of the words: 'If the Son therefore shall make you free, ye shall be free indeed.' One can sense that our Lord's teaching was too radical for the Pharisees, and it was in incidents like these that the seeds of opposition and conspiracy came to life, and bred, so that the Cross of Calvary became inevitable.

That, however, was about as far as our private thoughts could go, because the sound of the engine of our bus revving up, indicated that it was time to go into the town and relive in our imagination the events of the famous marriage which once took place in Cana of Galilee.

On the site of the house where Mary and Jesus once helped in the marriage celebrations, a church was built in the eighth century, and the present church was built on the same ground, which is now cared for by the Franciscans. So it is easy to let the imagination recreate the events recounted by St John. This is made the easier, in that ancient water pots and other authentic furnishings have been acquired. The antiquity of the crypt is enhanced by the display of museum pieces which date back to Roman times, but the main function of the site is to highlight its association with the marriage. This is done by the friars, who provide wine for the benefit of visitors — wine which they have made themselves.

The story of the first miracle which Jesus performed is well known. Mary, who was a close friend of the bridegroom's family discovered, to her consternation, that the supply of wine had run out. It was a crisis point, as far as the customs of wedding arrangements were concerned in those days. She came to Jesus, her son, and told Him what had happened. The reply He made is enigmatic to the reader, partly due to insufficient knowledge of the way He spoke, and the connotation of the phraseology of the times. His reply was, 'Your concern, Mother, is not mine. My hour has not yet come.' He certainly did not speak in terms of disrespect or rebuke, and we notice that Mary went to the servants and told them to do whatever He said. The words He used in Greek were, literally, 'What to me and thee?' 'Never mind' or 'Don't worry.' The verse as a whole very likely indicated that between them something could be worked out. Whatever the context of the words, his actions resolved the problem generously. The six water pots were filled with wine, which meant that they had ample supplies to meet the occasion. The Master of Ceremonies tasted the wine and was puzzled to know where it had come from. So, to the bridegroom he rushed, saying excitedly, 'Everyone serves the best wine first, and waits until the guests have drunk freely before serving the poorer sort; but you have kept the best wine until now.'

St John concludes the narrative by saying that this action at Cana of Galilee was the first of the signs by which Jesus revealed His glory and led His disciples to believe in Him. The miracle, happening on such an occasion as a wedding, when those involved were so anxious that nothing should go wrong with the arrangements, must have made a deep impression.

This story poses the question, how was it done? The simple answer is that we do not know. Some have felt that if we knew all the facts there would be no puzzlement. Attempts have been made to explain the miracle on a rational basis. In the end we are bound to take note that, amidst all the possibilities, it is impossible at such a distance from the time and circumstances to reconstruct the entire event. We bear in mind that the Son of Man and the Son of God is unique, and since His resurrection and its power is also a miracle, so we revere His earthly ministry which demonstrated His secret powers. He never performed a miracle to benefit Himself or to impress the spectator. Anything He did in this respect was to help someone else. The miracles bear the stamp of one who had an inner knowledge of the way God carries out His works of creation and providence. He understood the physical, mental and spiritual mechanism of humanity. In the handling of events, as in the spheres of healing and allied works, it is true that He saved others though eventually He could not save Himself.

Thinking over this incident, we discover an almost

inexhaustible wealth of material for preachers. This is partly
due to St John's genius for telling a story in a straightforward
way which is easily recalled, and at the same time providing
inner meanings and suggestions which are fascinating. This is
not the time to delve into these matters, but some of the
outstanding themes are worth mentioning. The Master's
presence at the marriage at Cana of Galilee has been used to
illustrate that Jesus was no kill-joy. He liked to see people
enjoying themselves. He felt it lay in the very nature of the
Gospel that they had every reason to be happy and outgoing.
Then, again, we can think of the homely associations of our
Lord throughout His earthly ministry. Above all, we cannot
miss the graciousness of His influence on those who turn to
Him for grace and salvation. It is always a turning of water
into wine.

We recall the incident at Bethany in the house of Simon the
leper. Here, again, we are in a home environment. Jesus and
His disciples had been invited for a meal and were enjoying it
when there was an unexpected interruption. A woman came
into the room, carrying a small bottle of very costly perfumed
oil which she proceeded to break open in order to anoint our
Lord's head. It was plainly an act of devotion, and intended to
demonstrate her indebtedness to Jesus and her deep
appreciation of all that He had done to help her and all that He
had been to her. This interruption was an annoyance to some
present, and they did not hesitate to voice their protest. 'Why
this waste? The perfume might have been sold for thirty
pounds, and the money given to the poor.' This hostile attitude
must have been a great shock to the woman, and, no doubt, the
atmosphere of the room had become tense. Jesus, however,
discerned the sacrifice she had made and the warmth of
devotion she was expressing. He sensed the sting of the critics'
words and so set out to redeem the situation. It is most likely
that the woman considered this to be the last opportunity of
offering a gift to her Lord, and, no doubt after much thought,
she decided upon the anointing. Jesus also knew that this
would be the last time this company of His Bethany friends
would be together with Him, so He took the tension out of the
atmosphere. Jesus said, 'Let her alone. Why must you make
trouble for her? It is a fine thing she has done for me. You have
the poor among you always, and you can help them whenever
you like, but you will not always have me. She has done what

lay in her power; she is beforehand with anointing my body for burial.' In this way Jesus turned the water into wine. In supporting her and understanding her he turned the cold water of criticism into the wine of appreciation. He revealed the importance of the gesture she had made. But He did something more. He placed this incident in the realm of the immortal. 'I tell you this,' He said, 'Wherever in all the world the Gospel is proclaimed, what she has done will be told as her memorial.' So it turned out to be. The situation was under His redeeming influence, and the water turned into wine.

Jesus was aware that He had come into this world with a special responsibility and a special calling, the establishment of the Kingdom of God and His rule. He was always alert to the will and intention of the Heavenly Father. He kept in mind the hour for which He had been sent. He never considered his own welfare, nor did He fail to perform the works of the Kingdom.

We always think of Cana of Galilee in association with the wedding, but there is another gracious act of our Lord linked to this little town. There was a certain nobleman whose son was ill at Capernaum. This man travelled with all haste to Cana and begged our Lord to come down and heal his son, who was at the point of death. Jesus said something which at first reading would have been likely to discourage the man, 'Except ye see signs and wonders ye will not believe.' Of course, these words might have been addressed to the spectators. However, the nobleman was too worried to be put off, and so with his anxiety showing in his voice and attitude, he said, 'Come down ere my child die.' His earnestness was an indication of the faith he had in Jesus, and the Master once more did the generous thing. Jesus said, 'Go thy way; thy son liveth'. The man believed the word that Jesus had spoken to him and he set out for Capernaum and home. Once more through the power of faith, Jesus had turned the water of anxiety into the wine of healing and joy.

St John must have had a warm place in his heart for Cana, for the reasons already evident, but also because it was the town from which Nathanael had come — Nathanael about whom our Lord said: 'Behold an Israelite indeed, in whom is no guile.' Nathanael wondered how Jesus knew him. Jesus had seen him standing under a fig tree and had sent Philip to invite him to join them. When Nathanael confessed Jesus to be the Son of God, Jesus' reply was: 'Because I said unto thee, I saw thee under the fig tree, believest thou? Thou shalt see greater things than these'. Nathanael did see greater things, and all the way it was turning the water into wine — transforming the mediocre into the inspiring.

In every human heart there is a thirst for something Christ is able to meet:

Those obstinate questionings
Of sense and outward things,
Fallings from us, vanishings;
Blank misgivings of a creature
Moving about in worlds not realised.

Wordsworth's words touch on the restlessness of the human heart. It is to the area of this restlessness and the worlds unrealised that Jesus leads the way as a good Shepherd. Along the highways and byways of His road, water keeps changing into wine.

27. THE HOUSE OF DATES

It is now time to go back to Jerusalem from whence we set out on our pilgrimage, and to bring that pilgrimage to a fitting conclusion by walking in the Master's footsteps, as He faced the final drama of His earthly ministry. Where better to begin than in the little village of Bethany where the home of Martha, Mary and Lazarus was always open to our Lord. It was with them He stayed during His visits to the city for the Passover occasions. Bethany is only about two and a half miles from Jerusalem, so the Master could travel to and from the city with ease. It was no doubt refreshing, after the noise and clamour of the streets which were crowded for the outstanding festivals, to leave the city and enjoy the cool of the evening among congenial friends who always provided warm-hearted hospitality. Jesus loved Martha, Mary and Lazarus and they must have been numbered among those whom the Scripture says He loved to the end.

Bethany is just a village (some would call it a hamlet), and it does not take long to see it all. We did not spend our time viewing the jumbled houses, but followed our guide up a steep street, with a wall on the left-hand side. We did not go very far before we came to a Church building, modern in style and dedicated to the names of Martha, Mary and Lazarus. There was a little door in the wall on the far side of the church, and there stood a woman, dressed in Arab costume. She had obviously considered this doorway to be a strategic point at which to stand, in the hope of selling her trinkets. A notice board stated in English that this was 'the tomb of Lazarus.' Once through the doorway, we descended by means of stone steps which wound their way down into the depths, ending in a little chamber with a stone slab where the body of Lazarus had lain. This recess, cut into the rock, looks ancient enough. While thinking of the raising of Lazarus from the dead unto life, one recalls the tradition that it was somewhere in this vicinity that Jesus was reputed to have made the statement 'I am the Resurrection and the Life; he that believeth in Me, though he were dead, yet shall he live.'

Near the tomb of Lazarus stands the little church which was built over the alleged site of the home of Martha, her sister and her brother. It was built in 1953 and presents a simplicity and beauty which is captivating. It stands there as a memorial to those close friends who must have felt most anxious for their Master's safety, especially on that last occasion when He was preparing to go into the city and face the ordeal that lay ahead. The three stained-glass windows portraying Martha, Mary and Lazarus not only appeal to the beholder's artistic sense, but turn the thoughts to the homely incident told by St Luke.

Jesus had come into the house, and, as the custom was, Martha set about preparing a meal. Jesus was seated, and Mary sat at His feet, discussing with Him the questions in her mind. Martha felt that Mary should be helping her and so she made her protest. Interrupting the flow of conversation, she said: — 'Lord, dost Thou not care that my sister hath left me to serve alone? Bid her therefore that she help me.' We notice that Martha addressed herself to Jesus, which would seem to indicate that she felt the Master was the one who was keeping Mary from rendering assistance. The Master's reply was both gracious and discerning. 'Martha, Martha, thou art careful and troubled about many things: But one thing is needful: and Mary hath chosen that good part, which shall not be taken from her.'

The issue here is not as is sometimes thought, between Martha, the practical, and Mary the contemplative. The fact that Martha expected Mary to lend a hand shows that Mary was accustomed to help in a practical way on such occasions. In addressing Jesus she seems to be putting the blame on Him. The issue involved in the homely scene of Martha appealing for help, of Mary, willing to help but absorbed in sharing the Master's thoughts, and of the Master's defence of Mary— the issue is a question of timing. There are times when we should drop the many ordinary things that hold our attention to provide an opportunity to sit at the feet of Jesus. Again the point here is not the conflict between work and worship. One can be certain that Martha was ready to sit at the Master's feet and Mary prepared to do the household chores. The need for a balance between work and worship is what comes to our attention as we examine this event in Bethany. Both work and worship ought to find expression in the business of life. God has created in human beings a fundamental urge to worship which should not be stifled, and the Son of God has taught us to implement that desire by making our daily work and service

THE ENTRANCE TO LAZARUS' TOMB

THE OLD JEWISH QUARTER IN JERUSALEM

the expression of worship — 'Inasmuch as ye have done it unto one of the least of these my brethren, ye have done it unto Me.'

Practice and contemplation should go together, the practical and the mystical should be balanced. There are times when there is a need to switch off the engine, to lift the foot from the accelerator, to be alert to wear and tear and to allow 'the peace of God which passeth all understanding' to seep into our souls. No amount of feverish activity should divert us from the opportunity of sitting at the feet of Jesus. Worship has its intrinsic value and is a necessary part of life. The worker has often been impatient with those who 'wait upon God', and certainly, without practical service the world could never keep turning. Yet we recall that Jesus never meant us to neglect the daily round, for He points out that God works, and so did He. The rhetorical question — 'For what is a man profited, if he shall gain the whole world, and lose his own soul?' — is worthy of sincere thought. That worship has its value is illustrated in that Jesus regarded it as the one thing needful and not to be taken away from Mary.

Taking one last glance at the illustrative windows in this modern little church in Bethany, we remembered that it was from this vicinity that our Lord organised His triumphal entry into Jerusalem. Mark and Luke both refer to Bethany and Bethphage, two neighbouring villages, as the place from which He set forth to demonstrate His Messiahship and His mission. The city of Jerusalem was filled with anticipation as the Passover time drew near. Rumours had circulated from Galilee, and in Jerusalem itself it was thought that the authorities were ready to move in and arrest Him. He had no illusions as to what was going on. He knew that His hour had come. The question on the lips of all who were visiting the temple was one of speculation. They were watching for Him everywhere, for it was common knowledge that the chief priests and Pharisees 'had given a commandment, that if any man knew where He was he should show it, that they might take him.' So the question on everybody's lips was — 'What think ye, that He will not come to the feast?'

28. THE MOUNT OF OLIVES

Now that his hour had come, our Lord made preparations for the last phase of His earthly ministry. It was to begin with the triumphal entry into the city of Jerusalem through the Golden Gate, and to end in the crucifixion at Calvary, just outside the old city walls. The events which took place, and which moved inexorably to their conclusion, happened quickly. From the triumphal entry to the resurrection was but a week — named Passion Week, because it produced the deep sorrows and sufferings of our Lord. As the prophet Isaiah had foretold, — 'He is despised and rejected of men; a man of sorrows, and acquainted with grief.'

The final drama began in Bethany and Bethphage, from which He turned in the direction of the Mount of Olives which lay between Him and the city. All four Gospels describe the spectacular entry. The Scriptures tell us that 'He steadfastly set his face to go to Jerusalem'. He knew what the pattern of His life was and He saw the Cross long beforehand. So much in His experience was linked with the prophets and their teaching that He could sense it all intuitively. Zechariah had said: 'Rejoice greatly, O daughter of Zion; shout, O daughter of Jerusalem; behold, thy king cometh unto thee; he is just and having salvation; lowly and riding upon an ass, and upon a colt, the foal of an ass.' Jesus now proclaimed openly the nature of His person and His mission to the world.

His preparation was thorough and He planned well in advance. He had arranged through a good friend to borrow a beast of burden, and when the time came to use the animal, He sent two of His disciples to the nearby village to fetch it. If anyone were to ask them what they were doing they were merely to say, 'The Lord hath need of him.' On Palm Sunday, the whole stage was set. The chief priests, scribes and Pharisees had formed their conspiracy to have Jesus arrested, though at the time they had to step warily because He was still popular with the common people. Many ardent followers had come from Galilee to the Passover. No doubt His movements were noted. Pilate had taken up residence in Jerusalem, having come to the capital of Judaea from his headquarters in Caesarea on the Mediterranean coast. The garrison was augmented for the occasion, lest trouble should erupt. Aware of all this, our Lord appreciated the gathering of His friends in Bethany, and in His secret heart He was pondering on deep and immortal thoughts.

All through His earthly ministry He was conscious of the hour of His Cross. People were always asking if He were the Messiah or not. From his prison cell, John the Baptist sent some of His disciples to ask Jesus:'Art Thou He that should come, or do we look for another.' Our Lord's reply was, 'Go and show John again those things which ye do hear and see; the blind receive their sight, and the lame walk, the lepers are cleansed, and the deaf hear, the dead are raised up and the poor have the Gospel preached to them.' The evidence of His Messiahship should have been clear in these events which had been prophesied. Yet all along there was a demand that He should say clearly, 'I am the Messiah.' Jesus, however, preferred that the Spirit of God should lead them to discern His nature through His work and influence. This was the method He chose at Caesarea Philippi when He asked, 'Whom do men say that I am?' It was Peter who brought joy to His heart when he replied, 'Thou art the Christ, the Son of the living God.' Jesus went on to say: 'Blessed art thou, Simon Bar-jona; for flesh and blood hath not revealed it unto thee, but my Father which is in Heaven.' Now He was to make a public declaration affirming His Messiahship, which the people would understand.

On His instructions, the colt was brought to Him and the rumour spread like wild-fire that Jesus of Nazareth was on His way to the city. The crowds of pilgrims gathered, and by the time they had reached the Mount of Olives there was an impressive gathering which grew in number as they moved in the direction of the city. This was Jesus' answer to the question, 'What think ye, that He will not come to the feast?'

Before we went to Israel, no doubt we had imaginative pictures in our mind of the Mount of Olives. We might have thought in terms of a miniature forest of grey-green olive trees covering the slopes. In reality it is not just like that. Olive trees there are, but not in profusion. The slopes of the Mount are not dotted with clumps of olive, but churches, built to commemorate some aspect of our Lord's presence there, and other buildings,

now break up the belt of trees. Among the churches we see the
Church of Dominus Flevit, the Church of all Nations and the
Russian Church of St Mary Magdalene.

In the time of our Lord, however, it was different. The Mount
could be more truly called the Mount of Olives because its
terraced and rocky slopes were covered with olive trees.

The reason for the change can be traced back to events which
took place shortly after the time of our Lord. The Romans had
dominated this outpost of their empire for years, and the
inhabitants of Judaea deeply resented their presence. They
wanted Rome to withdraw its army and leave them to rule
themselves. The local people turned to revolt from time to time,
but the Roman legions were too strong for them. In the middle
of the sixth decade of the first century A.D., the inhabitants of
Jeruslalem and the surrounding countryside had an idea that
the time was ripe for another revolt, and that they could force
the Romans to leave Judaea. Accordingly they organised their
forces and made a sharp attack upon their masters. At first
they met with some success to which Nero, the Emperor,
reacted as one would expect. He decided that the inhabitants of
Jerusalem needed a lesson. He commissioned Titus, one of his
most successful generals, to set out with an adequate army to
crush the rebellion and destroy the city.

Commanding an army of four legions, the Fifth, Tenth,
Twelfth and Fifteenth, supported by cavalry, auxiliary troops,
battering rams and *ballistae* (giant catapults for projecting
huge stones) he set about his invasion with typical Roman
thoroughness. Jerusalem was reduced to rubble, the walls torn
down, the temple destroyed and our Lord's prophecy, 'See ye
not these things? (referring to the temple) Verily I say unto you,
there shall not be left here one stone upon another, that shall
not be thrown down' — fulfilled in no uncertain manner.

When the campaign was successfully completed, Titus left
the Tenth Legion to set up their quarters on the Mount of
Olives. He intended to make certain that the Jews would not
attempt to rebuild the city. This legion thought nothing of
cutting down the olive trees, using the wood for scaling ladders,
camp fires and many other purposes. Strangely enough eight
trees survived and they are in the Garden of Gethsemane. They
have special significance for the Christian pilgrims and
tourists who go there every year. So, standing on the Mount of
Olives we can picture in our imaginations the simplicity of the

procession of Palm Sunday, which was a different kind of advance from that of Titus which displayed the gleam of armour and helmets, tunics and cloaks with flashes of red and gold. The Jewish war, which began in A.D. 66 and ended with the devastation of Jerusalem in A.D. 70, has left a mark on the Mount of Olives which can still be seen after almost two thousand years. The olive trees have found it difficult to be fully reinstated.

We pick up the story of Palm Sunday, with Jesus descending the Mount of Olives, crossing the Kedron stream and making his way towards what is now called the Golden Gate, which is thought to be built on the place where Jesus entered the city in pomp and circumstance.

They placed garments on top of the colt and Jesus sat thereon. A procession, entering into the spirit and the significance of the occasion, took up position, some walking in front, and others forming the rear, with our Lord in the centre. Many spread their garments in the way, and as they moved forward past Gethsemane and over the Kedron, they took up the prophetic cry, 'Hosanna; Blessed is He that cometh in the name of the Lord: Hosanna in the highest.'

The procession moved up the hill toward the gate into the city. Here we see an imposing double gate with two round arches crowned with small domes. The Golden Gate received its name in honour of the occasion when the Emperor Heraclius passed through it, celebrating his victory over the Russians in A.D. 739. The top of the Gateway is battlemented like the rest of the wall into which it is built, but it rises above it in such a way as to catch the eye. The two Roman arches are supported on either side and in the middle by three Corinthian pillars, and the remaining facade is neatly decorated with rectangles and circles.

We are not told much in the Gospel narrative as to what actually took place while Jesus was entering the city. Those who were already in the city were curious to know what the commotion was about. The question on their lips was, 'Who is this?' The reply they were given was, 'This is Jesus, the prophet of Nazareth of Galilee.' Nevertheless it was a Messianic demonstration, and, as such, was not lost on the authorities. Jesus, nonetheless, was coming in peace and the programme He had in mind was reconciliation. On the other hand, He had no illusions, for we learn from St Luke that as He drew near to the city His pent-up feelings broke loose into tears, 'If thou hadst known, even thou, in this thy day, the things which belong unto thy peace! but now they are hid from thine eyes. For the days shall come upon thee, that thine enemies shall cast a trench about thee, and compass thee round, and keep thee in on every side, and they shall lay thee even with the ground, and thy children within thee; and they shall not leave in thee one stone upon another; because thou knowest not the time of thy visitation.' So Jesus foresaw the destruction of His beloved city, and by A.D. 70 the prophecy was fulfilled.

Because of the popularity of Jesus among the common people at the time, and the demonstration of the trust they placed in Him, and the significance they attached to His entry into the city, the Pharisees felt it prudent not to lay hands on Him yet. Nevertheless, they expressed their opposition by asking Him to rebuke His followers. In reply Jesus said, 'I tell you that, if these should hold their peace, the stones would immediately cry out.' Jesus knew there was a conspiracy afoot to destroy Him, but by now His mind was made up and He was prepared to see His work carried through to the end.

The procession broke up. The people mingled with the crowd. Jesus spent some time in Jerusalem showing particular interest in what was going on in the temple. That night He returned to Bethany to rest after an exhausting day.

It would be very tempting to walk fully in the Master's footsteps during the last week of His earthly ministry, but when one follows the events, it is clear that this would be beyond the terms of reference as far as this book is concerned. Since we have in mind visitors to the Holy Land whose main object is to look through as many windows as possible in a very limited time, it would be more practical to describe the sites associated with Passion Week rather than to go into the historical events in detail. Furthermore, the pilgrims and tourists would be familiar with the events through their knowledge of the New Testament.

On the day following the excitement of the triumphal entry of Palm Sunday, Jesus returned to Jerusalem and again visited the temple, causing a stir by an act of reformation. He cleared out the money changers and those who traded in sacrificial birds and animals — overturning their stalls and proclaiming, 'My house shall be called the house of prayer; but ye have made it a den of thieves.' (A reference to the extortion imposed upon the pilgrims). In keeping with the heart of the matter, He went on to do the work of social and spiritual healing, since people were very important to Him. The blind and the lame were not far away wherever He appeared. Presumably He returned to Bethany at the close of the day. On Tuesday He was back at the temple where He spent the day teaching and discussing questions. Much of His instruction was in parabolic form, and as for the questions, many of them were of a controversial nature and loaded with danger if He gave the wrong answer. There were questions regarding the Jewish people paying tribute money to their Roman overlords. Since the money involved bore the inscription of Caesar, He countered the subtlety of His questioners with the words, 'Render therefore unto Caesar the things which are Caesar's; and unto God the things which are God's.' Then there were the religious questions concerning John the Baptist. Was he a prophet of God or just an ordinary man? What standing had he and by what authority did Jesus Himself carry out the revolutionary work in which He was engaged? Jesus answered their questions with another question, 'I will ask you one thing, which if ye tell me, I, in like wise, will tell you by what authority I do these things. The baptism of John, was it from God, or from men?' The reply did not come spontaneously, since it involved a trap — 'If we say "From God", He will say, "Then why did you not believe him?" But if we say, "From men", we are afraid of the people.' The common people had accepted John as a prophet. So they answered evasively — 'We do not know.' Then Jesus informed them that He would not tell them (as He had said) by what authority He acted.

In another temple incident, our Lord showed deep appreciation of the gesture of a widow giving a mite toward the offering. 'I tell you this,' He said, 'this widow hath given more than any of the others; for those others who have given had more than enough, but she, with less than enough, has given all that she had to live on.'

During the Tuesday and again on the Wednesday He continued teaching and getting in as much work as possible, since the time was short. Yet in the midst of all the activity there was one special meeting He was secretly organising. He wanted one last meeting with His disciples before He would face the Cross. The disciples themselves were thinking in terms of the Passover, but Jesus had a new development in mind. He made private arrangements with a good friend in the city to have the use of his upper room for the occasion. The request was willingly granted. Our Lord's deepest desire was that He should have the opportunity of joining with these men whom He had chosen in Galilee, and who had given up their employment to serve Him in the work of the Kingdom of God. 'Having loved his own which were in the world, he loved them unto the end.'

Time was fast running out, so He gave instructions to two of His disciples to go into the city and to follow a man who would be carrying a pitcher of water, and to ask the man of the house to which he would lead them, 'Where is the guestchamber, where I shall eat the Passover with my disciples? And he shall show you a large upper room furnished; there make ready.' Jesus and the other disciples would arrive later under cover of darkness. Already the nets were closing. Judas was carrying out his betrayal plans. The authorities had posted their men to watch for Him. The succeeding events followed the pattern our Lord had in mind, and in the Upper Room the sacrament of the Lord's Supper was instituted. The disciples, and all who would believe in Him eventually through their witness, were to remember Him and the significance of His death by the breaking of bread and the sharing of the cup.

Our guide led us to an upper room by means of a stairway. At this point in time it is not easy to establish whether this is authentic or not. One argument is that when the early Christians were scattered for one reason or another they always knew the sites of their dearest memories and returned to the old places to rebuild and continue the traditions. If we accept this it is possible to argue that we were indeed on the site of the Upper Room and that the style of its appearance has been maintained.

The room we entered was indeed a large upper room with sturdy pillars supporting the roof. On the day we visited it there were no less than three parties present, and there was adequate room for all. One party was from South America, another from Germany and we were from the North of Ireland. Each group assembled in different corners and held a very simple Communion Service of their own. A sincere spirit of reverence descended upon everyone as we shared a little bread and wine and meditated upon the Last Supper. An outstanding feature of the simple service was that by chance and not design, the three groups said the Lord's Prayer simultaneously. Though none of the parties knew the language of the others, we knew we were saying the same prayer and sensed instinctively that in this we were one. While we came from different backgrounds and traditions, we felt the common bond of one Shepherd and one Fold. That we were all one in Christ Jesus was evidenced in the smiles we exchanged when we left the Upper Room to make way for other groups seeking an entrance. One may think of the numbers of people who have visited this room throughout the centuries. They must amount to millions. It was a privilege to pass that way and to think of that night when Jesus washed the feet of His disciples and spoke of the broken body and the shed blood.

This would be as good a point as any to turn to the Church of Paternoster, a modern building quite close to the city and on a hillside. It is built over a Crusader Church of the twelfth century, commemorating the teaching of the Lord's prayer to His disciples when they said:, 'Lord, teach us to pray.' When we arrived at the entrance we were attracted by an Arab, dressed in full regalia, holding the reins of a decoratively attired camel.

He invited us to mount the camel and have a shaky ride. Many of our party did so and paid the required money. When the courageous were safely lodged in the saddle and had enjoyed a short and comparatively gentle ride on a circular course, the Arab held the animal still for sufficient time to allow all concerned to take photographs. When the fun of the sideshow was over, we entered the precincts of the Church. Here we found ourselves in cloistered corridors divided into sections by pillars, and on the inner wall of each compartment was a mural. Each mural consisted of the Lord's prayer written in one of the languages of many of the nations of the world. The lettering was decorative and artistic and a separate section was given to each presentation. We were able to follow the French, the Latin, and to a little extent, the German; the English was easy and the Gaelic reminded us of our native land. The 'Our Father' could be read in sixty-three languages altogether, including Hebrew, Arabic, Russian, Armenian, and Dutch. A close study of the lettering and design of each revealed a high standard of workmanship and dedication.

As the guide led us underground to a fairly spacious cave which receded into the natural rock, he said, 'It was here that Jesus taught the disciples The Prayer, the prayer that has become the common heritage of all Christendom.' We noticed a small window, or grille, in the wall, which revealed a passageway leading beyond the cave. Evidently it led to the quarter where a band of nuns exercised the special responsibility of caring for the site, the preservation and upkeep of the Church. They were not to be seen or heard, and we were told that once a year they could come to the barred window and speak to their relatives and friends.

Standing there in the midst of the display of so many languages, my first thought was the universality of the Lord's Prayer. From east to west, from north to south, around the continents of the world, human lips were uttering, and human hearts praying this prayer. Whether one lived under the shadow of the Rockies, the wilderness of the Australian outback or in the heart of a great capital city on any of the continents, here is a prayer for each and all — a prayer that has universal appeal. If sixty-three people from all the countries represented on the murals were assembled in one room and did not know one another's language, they would sense a common bond of communication in repeating the Lord's Prayer. Human nature being the same the world over, people would find common ground in the words 'Our Father' and cherish the vision and experience that the title suggests. In its brevity it is in keeping with our Lord's own thoughts of the close relationship between the Heavenly Father and His children. 'Use not vain repetition as the heathen do; for they think they shall be heard for their much speaking; Be not therefore like unto them: For your Heavenly Father knoweth what things ye have need of, before ye ask Him.' When one thinks of these words, they reveal an intimate personal relationship in which a human being can believe that the Father is working beyond our knowledge and appreciation.

As we left the Church of Paternoster, we saw the Arab and his camel still making a living. The camel was kneeling down to allow an American tourist to return to *terra firma*. The lady had evidently enjoyed herself, judging by her infectious laughter. As for the camel, it was noticeable that God had so made him that he knelt down to receive his burden, and he also knelt down to get rid of it. Perhaps the camel can teach us something here.

We look across the valley to the Holy City, and return in thought to the Upper Room which prompted our digression to the Church of Paternoster. When the Last Supper had ended, our Lord uttered some final words to His disciples for their comfort, enlightenment, encouragement and consolation. These are recorded in St John's Gospel in chapter fourteen. Death is not the end. 'Let not your heart be troubled; ye believe in God, believe also in me. In my Father's house are many mansions — I go to prepare a place for you.' Instead of His physical presence, they would have the spiritual presence of the Holy Spirit to sustain and guide them. Finally they were assured of His legacy — 'Peace I leave with you, my peace I give unto you. Let not your heart be troubled, neither let it be afraid.' It was what the apostle Paul has called 'the peace of God which passeth all understanding'. The peace deep down in the heart which the world cannot touch or take away! The peace which comes while we struggle on in faith, facing up to the realities of life rather than running away from them.

As we pass on from the thoughts of the Upper Room, we spare a thought for what the immediate future held for Jesus and the little band of disciples. They walked out into the night — the Shepherd to be arrested and crucified, and the sheep scattered.

30. GETHSEMANE

If the names Bethlehem and Galilee cast a spell on the imagination the same applies to Gethsemane — the place of agony and betrayal. The name itself means oilpress, and the association with the olive trees is apparent when one scans the Mount of Olives. The fact that eight olive trees survived the Roman occupation during the assault on Jerusalem in A.D. 70, and are alive today to give the devout some touch of the atmosphere when Jesus knelt in Gethsemane in His agonising prayer, adds deeper significance to the name. The Garden of Gethsemane is a walled-in section of the Mount, nestling on its lower slopes. It was to this favourite haunt that our Lord repaired on the Thursday night of Passion Week.

The garden itself must not have changed very much from the days when our Lord looked upon these trees. They are so old that quite a deep hollow has formed in the heart of each trunk, while the trees live on and new olive roots spring from the old ones so that fresh branches spread out. Thus the trees survive. The garden is cared for by the Franciscan Order who carefully protect this sacred plot. The necessity for protection explains why it is contained by a wall. While one sits, or walks, or stands in contemplation among these ancient trees it is awe-inspiring to feel a secret rapport with the events of that night when Jesus prepared Himself for the final and irrevocable step of self-sacrifice.

Near to the garden is the Church of All Nations, so-called because many nations undertook each to be responsible for a portion of the Church. One of its distinctive features is the series of domes on the roof. Each dome crowns that part of the Church which the particular nation undertook to construct. The combined effort of different nations engaged in building this early twentieth-century Church, reminds us of the words of Scripture used by Handel in his musical interpretation of the Messiah, 'The kingdoms of this world are become the kingdoms of our Lord, and of His Christ; and He shall reign for ever and ever.' How richly does Jesus deserve this honour, we felt, as we looked at a section of protruding rock, enclosed by a circle of wrought iron work artistically fashioned to represent the crown

of thorns. His had to be the crown of thorns, symbolising the
agony He must have felt as He knelt down upon the rock,
pouring out His soul unto God that if possible the cup of
suffering might pass from Him. Yet in His heart of hearts he
knew the crown of thorns had to be accepted. So He ended His
searching prayer with the words, 'Nevertheless, not my will,
but thine be done.'

Having resigned Himself to the inevitable Cross, Jesus
returned to Peter, James and John whom He had left in a state
of confusion, bewilderment and exhaustion while He went
apart for prayer. He found them deep in sleep, because in their
weariness nature had taken over. As He looked on them one can
surely trace infinite pity, deep sorrow and gracious
understanding, as He said 'Sleep on now, and take your rest';
like a mother feeling for her children, who sleep in the midst of
some tragedy, not fully aware of the real nature of the crisis.
But the prayer had served its purpose; the events were
beginning to move and the disciples had a rude awakening. The
silence of the garden was shattered. A contingent of soldiers,
together with a crowd of people, excited with the anticipation of
drama, had been led by Judas, one of the twelve, to the Master.
The swords and staves were unnecessary. Jesus was now
simply following the dictation of events as He accepted His
destiny. St Luke records the Master's words to Judas,
'Judas, betrayest thou the Son of man with a kiss?'

Gethsemane — the Garden of so many happy memories, is
now associated with the painful agony of our Lord. The whole
drama demonstrates how man in his irresponsibility often
turns to chaos and destruction the loveliest things God offers to
him. Some sinister force within him drives him to foul his own
nest.

Taking a last walk round the Garden we wandered towards
the Russian Church of St Mary Magdalene, built a short
distance up the hill from Gethsemane. It was built in the
nineteenth century, and its attractive feature is its
onion-shaped dome. We ponder in our hearts on Mary
Magdalene and all those other folks who had reason to rejoice
in the knowledge of the redeeming grace of God, and we find
much satisfaction that such grace is open to us still.

Continuing our thoughts on Passion Week, we watch Jesus,
now arrested, being led captive over the Kedron and up the
slopes toward the city. Since the chief priests, elders and scribes

had been responsible for enlisting the help of the army to secure Jesus' arrest, and their conspiracy had at last succeeded, it was only natural that He should be taken to them. St John tells us that He was taken to Annas first. Annas had been the high priest, but the office had passed on to Caiaphas. Now Caiaphas was the son-in-law of Annas, so that Annas held considerable influence and power still. However, it was Caiaphas' responsibility to find the grounds he needed to put Jesus to death and to substantiate a case against Him that the Roman authorities could accept and approve. St John also tells us that two of His disciples had mingled with the crowd that multiplied as news of Jesus' arrest circulated. One was Peter, who followed at a distance. The other disciple is not named, but since John, in his Gospel, often refers to 'the disciple whom Jesus loved,' that disciple is most likely to have been John. As for the rest of the disciples, they had scattered and fled in panic — which is understandable in the severe stress of the hour. One feels that Jesus had allowed for this when, a little earlier, He had prophesied, 'Behold the hour cometh, yea, is now come, that ye shall be scattered, every man to his own, and shall leave me alone.'

Annas interviewed our Lord, while waiting for the Sanhedrin to gather in the palace of Caiaphas. Here we come across another of these doubles, where there are different traditions concerning the sites. One tradition places the House of Caiaphas just outside the Zion Gate at the southern wall where an American monastery now stands. Here, it is alleged, Jesus was imprisoned, and it was in this vicinity that the cock crew. The other tradition claims the location to be a little further outside the southern wall and to the east of the Cenaculum, the name given to the Church built on the site of the house of Mary, mother of John Mark, who is associated with one of our Lord's resurrection appearances and the event of Pentecost. On the slopes of Mount Zion to the east stands the Church of St Peter in Gallicantu — 'Church of the Cock-crowing', and this Church is alleged to be built on the site of Caiaphas' palace. Whichever one visits, it does not prevent meditation upon the events as they moved swiftly towards the crucifixion of our Lord. While Jesus was being questioned, and witnesses were being sought to testify against Him, Peter was going through a harrowing experience. He was accused of being one of Jesus' disciples by a maid who recognised him while he was sitting near to a fire.

Vehemently he protested, and denied that he had any
association with the prisoner. At this point the cock crew, and
Jesus, still being conducted in captivity, turned and looked at
Peter. Peter recalled the words of the Master, 'Before the cock
crows, thou shalt deny me thrice.' The big fisherman went out
and wept bitterly. The Master's look, however, was not one of
condemnation, but of understanding and forgiveness. It
prompted Peter to become what Jesus had once called him, the
rock upon which He would build His Church.

The chief priests, the elders and all the council failed to find
satisfactory witnesses to ensure our Lord's condemnation,
other than two false witnesses who maintained that He had
said He was able to destroy the temple of God, and to build it in
three days. When questioned about His Messiahship, He
annoyed them with the words, 'Thou hast said: nevertheless I
say unto you, hereafter shall ye see the Son of man sitting on
the right hand of power, and coming in the clouds of heaven.' St
Mark tells us that in answer to the question, 'Art thou the
Christ, the Son of the Blessed?' Jesus said, 'I am.' So the high
priest rent his clothes, proclaimed he had spoken blasphemy
and asked for the council's decision. They said, 'He is worthy of
death.' They spat in His face, buffeted Him, slapped Him with
their hands and took Him to Pilate, the Roman Governor, who
alone could order the death penalty. The New Testament
evangelists record that in the background, Judas was already
feeling the consequences of our Lord's words, 'Truly the Son of
man goeth, as it was determined: but woe unto that man by
whom he is betrayed!' Judas received his betrayal money, but it
proved worthless. His reaction to his treachery led to deep
remorse, ending in suicide.

The visitor to Jerusalem has the opportunity of walking up
the very steps which Jesus trod when He was taken from the
Sanhedrin's Council Chambers to the fortress of Antonia,
where Pilate exercised his authority as Roman Governor with
jurisdiction over all Judaea. This stairway up the side of the hill
is typical of Roman building. Although so ancient, it is in good
repair and is likely to last for many, many centuries to come,
unless some catastrophe intervenes. The steps rise gently and
are wide, so that the ascent is not so exhausting as it otherwise
would be. When we were ascending this ancient stairway, we
were literally walking in the footsteps of the Master.

Returning to the sequence of events, we see Jesus led into the

presence of Pilate. The hall in which He was judged was close to
the Fortress Antonia which had been built by Herod the Great
in A.D.25, and was where Pilate had established his
Praetorium. Here were his well-chosen guards. Since the
Passover had drawn people from all over Judaea, Galilee and
further afield, Pilate and his best troops had taken up residence
in the city, where they could keep a watchful eye on the temple
and its surrounds, and be ready to quell any disorders that
might occur. The trial of Jesus before Pilate probably took place
in the judgement hall of the Praetorium. Our guide led us to the
courtyard and directed our attention to the serrated stone floor,
which was polished to some extent by the hooves of the horses
of the Roman cavalry who rode in and out freely. The
indentations on the floor surface had been worked by design to
provide a grip for the horses' hooves and prevent them from
slipping. Another interesting feature is a scratched-out design
on the floor, for a game played by the Roman soldiers, when on
guard. Often the stakes were the lives of some of the prisoners.
This gambling game, played on the large flagstones, was called
the Game of Kings. As one stands among the marble Roman
pillars, and is shown the one to which Jesus is alleged to have
been bound, and there scourged, one recalls the whole sordid
scene of the mockery of the soldiers who found entertainment in
putting a 'royal' robe on Him, a crown of thorns on His head
and a reed as 'sceptre' in His hand, bowing in jest before Him
and intoning, 'Hail! King of the Jews.'

While reading the accounts of the trial of Jesus first by the
Sanhedrin and then before Pilate, we notice a crucial change in
the charge. In the former, Jesus was condemned on a charge of
blasphemy, but the accusations before Pilate were of a different
nature. To suit the desire for our Lord's condemnation, they
switched from the religious approach to the political, although
the two spheres overlapped. Matthew and Mark give similar
testimony to this change. The emphasis here was on the loaded
political question asked by the governor, 'Art thou the King of
the Jews?' This thought had been in the Roman mind before. St
John tells us that at one point earlier in our Lord's ministry, the
extreme nationalists would have taken Jesus by force to make
Him a king, but Jesus had eluded them. Now the question was
on the lips of Pilate, to test whether there was a case of treason
and a move to rebel against Caesar. St Luke adds that those
who were seeking permission for the death penalty kept saying,

'We found this fellow perverting the nation, and forbidding to give tribute to Caesar, saying that He Himself is Christ, a king.'

Pilate had some difficulty in finding substantial evidence on these accusations, and he urged them to produce something valid. At this point they exhausted his patience by replying with acrimony rather than with logic, 'If he were not a malefactor, we would not have delivered him up unto thee.' Nonetheless, the Roman governor made a further attempt to find some way of resolving the problem. He questioned Jesus more closely on the issue of kingship, and the answer which Jesus gave cleared the air for Pilate, 'My kingdom is not of this world: if my kingdom were of this world, then would my servants fight, that I should not be delivered to the Jews.' It was at the end of this interview that, in perplexity, Pilate asked the rhetorical question, 'What is truth?' (In his essay on truth, Francis Bacon reflects that he did not stay for an answer.) Instead he thought of a way out of the impasse.

Facing the Jewish multitude, he pointed out that at the Passover there was a custom whereby a prisoner should be given his freedom as a gesture to the occasion. There was a notable prisoner at hand called Barabbas, and he gave them a choice — 'the King of the Jews', or Barabbas. With one voice they opted for Barabbas. Now, placed in an unenviable position, Pilate had to make a decision. Since he could find nothing worthy of death in Jesus, being aware of His sincerity and innocence, and knowing full well that Jesus was not seeking an earthly throne or to overthrow the sovereignty of Rome, he could not bring himself to pronounce the death sentence against all Roman justice. His uneasiness was further increased when his wife sent a message not to have anything to do with this just man. Be that as it may, the mood of the multitude was electric and their raucous cries were bloodthirsty. In an effort to keep the peace at all costs, he succumbed to the threatening words, 'If thou lettest this man go, thou art not Caesar's friend; whosoever maketh himself a king speaketh against Caesar.'

Pilate had tried everything. When he had urged Herod to hear the case because Jesus was a Galilean, he had been grasping at a straw. Herod would have none of it. Accordingly, Pilate took water and washed his hands in the sight of the multitude, saying, 'I am innocent of the blood of this just person; see ye to it.' He handed him over. 'They took Jesus and led him away.'

Pontius Pilate had made his decision with grave misgiving. In a narrow street of old Jerusalem one is shown a small section of an overhead arch — the 'Ecce Homo' arch — marking the place where Pilate said to the Jews, 'Behold the Man.'

The soldiers who had been mocking Jesus took off the 'royal' robe from Him and dressed Him in his own robe. They now led Him away to be crucified. Round about three o'clock every Friday the Franciscans lead pilgrims along the Way of Sorrows (Via Dolorosa), and seek to share, in a dramatic way, the painful walk to Calvary. Their destination is the Church of the Holy Sepulchre, which is said to embrace Golgotha and the tomb where the body of Jesus was laid. The sepulchre had been offered by Joseph of Arimathea who had originally purchased it for his own burial place, but counted it a privilege to give it to his Lord. When he sought permission later to take down the body of Jesus from the Cross, the request was granted and our Lord was lovingly cared for.

The Church of the Holy Sepulchre serves as a very useful place of devotion and meditation, but the visitor to the Holy Land must leave aside any preconceived ideas of seeing a silhouetted outline of the hill called Calvary and the sense of space that goes with it, for the Church stands in a built up area. There is an enormous rock wall, forming part of the hill and, incidently, showing an impressive split from top to bottom, reminiscent of the earthquake and the rending of rocks mentioned in the Gospels. The Church stands today, virtually unchanged from the days of the Crusaders. One wall is decorated in a most unusual way. Each Crusader, visiting the sacred site, carved a single little cross to mark the occasion and to pay homage to his Lord. The wall is completely covered with these decorative crosses, and when one stands looking at them, the imagination can see the Crusaders, each working one as his own personal tribute to the Lord whose name he sought to honour.

It is quite a contrast to walk from the bright sunshine of the courtyard into the Church, where one is enveloped in 'a dim religious light'. Pilgrims and tourists from all over the world, and wearing different national dress, are moving in and out endlessly. There are little chapels clustered round the tomb of Christ to which visitors may repair for meditation and prayer, each according to his own tradition. The observer becomes very much aware of the wide variety of expressions there are of the

Christian faith. Eastern Orthodox, Copts, Armenians and Catholics and many more communions repair to their chosen corner. There are lamps, tinselly ornaments, valuable pieces, gaudy decorations and a wide variety of icons, artistic tapestries and allied forms of devotion. These represent the love and appreciation of the many branches of the Vine. Each branch, holding central sites within the area, has its established rights, and these are diligently safeguarded.

Having a natural sympathy for the underdog, my heart went out to the Abyssinian monks who had once possessed more advantageous quarters inside the Church, but who had been gradually edged upwards and out on to the roof. Here they live right on top of the massive structure. Their huts or dwellings are primitive enough, and they have a small chapel which can only accommodate a few at a time. One of their peculiar rituals is to go in search of the body of Christ, demonstrating the fact that it cannot be found: 'He is not here; He is risen.' We tried to communicate with some of these monks, who were doing their daily chores. They had a warm smile for us, as indeed we had for them, but alas, both sides had to rely simply on friendly attitudes and gestures, for we were unable to cross the language barrier.

Right at the heart of all the religious fervour of the Church of the Holy Sepulchre is the tomb itself. The dimness of the area is brightened by a galaxy of candles, and the tomb itself is illumined by a number of oriental hanging lamps. The sepulchre is a small rectangular cell. On the right hand side, as one enters, is a stone which has been covered by a marble slab. From a marble roof hang the lamps which are supplied by Latin, Greek, Coptic and Armenian groups. A bearded monk was on duty, limiting the number of people entering so that there would be no overcrowding at any given time. He also attended to their devotional needs if required. There was a steady stream of men and women coming and going. All the other passages and tunnels, chapels and oratories radiated from the tomb area.

We moved out of the Church of the Holy Sepulchre into the bright light of the courtyard, sat down on a stone seat, which runs along the side of it, to take one last look at the place which is called Calvary, and thought of that evening when the Son of man and the Son of God lifted up His voice and cried, 'My God, my God, why hast Thou forsaken me.' St John adds the three words which round off the drama and tragedy of that hour, 'It is finished.' The work of grace and salvation had been completed by way of the Cross. it was a demonstration to the world that God so loved the world that He gave His only begotten Son, that whosoever would believe in Him should not perish but have everlasting life.

Rising from our seats, we walked into the workaday world once again, with shopkeepers handing out cups of thick coffee to prospective buyers; greengrocers drawing attention to their alluring melons, grapefruits, oranges and pomegranates; the scramble of human beings trying to make their voices heard; the occasional jostling to make way for a man and his donkey or mule. No motor traffic in this part of the old city! David Street is so narrow, that it makes no friendly gesture toward the automobile, and stone steps of all depths and widths are necessary for movement from one level to another. One question rose in our minds. Was Calvary not supposed to be outside the walls? Did we not sing:

There is a green hill far away,
Without a city wall
Where the dear Lord was crucified
Who died to save us all.

Yet the Church of the Holy Sepulchre is obviously inside the walls. There is a satisfactory answer to this query. Herod the Great strengthened the northern wall for defence reasons, and built the three towers of Antonia, Hippicus and Phasaelus. At that time the northern wall was further south than the present one, and so Golgotha, represented by the site of the Holy Sepulchre, was then outside the northern wall. However, the question is allied to another of those doubles which make for a little controversy with regard to some of the sacred sites. What is called the Garden Tomb is also suggested as the location of Calvary and the Sepulchre. So we go across to the north-east of the city and seek another site which is definitely outside the walls — even the present north wall. Let us then take a look through another window and consider the Garden Tomb.

31. THE GARDEN TOMB

We had been walking along a busy street in the city, absorbing the insistent noise of the traffic, tolerating the drone of motor car engines, enduring the hooting of horns, when we came to a gateway. Passing through it, we seemed to be in another world. As we walked further along the path in front of us the city sounds seemed to retreat and we were conscious of the scent and beauty of flower and shrub, the shadow of trees and all that we associate with a peaceful and colourful garden. As we rounded a corner, we were forced to stand still by a remarkable scene confronting us. It was a hill which rose gradually from the left hand side of our vision to a rounded top, and then plunged steeply on the right. It was then we noticed three deep holes on the face of the hill and quite involuntarily someone said: 'Golgotha—the place of a skull!'

From the natural features of this hill, it is well-nigh impossible not to be excited by thoughts of Calvary. Sure enough, it suggested ideas of the hill outside the city wall 'where the dear Lord was crucified.' There, in stark clarity, stood a hill which had the features of a skull. As we examined it more closely from our vantage point, it was almost uncanny how suitable this site could have been for a crucifixion. The Cross of Jesus, together with those of the two condemned criminals on either side would stand out, silhouetted against the sky, and as many people as desired to come would have gained a grandstand view. The spectators lined along the ground on which we were standing, would have had an uninterrupted view as they looked upwards to the top of the hill. Calvary was just high enough to display every detail of the crucifixion, and near enough to allow the voices of those involved in the tragedy to be heard. The hill face was almost sheer, so that no one would have been anxious to climb this side in front of us. The approach up the gentle slope from the left would have allowed the soldiers and the condemned to take their places. There was ample room round the Cross for both those who had chosen to be there, and those who had simply come for the entertainment of a spectacle. St Luke tells us that 'the people stood beholding. And the rulers also with them derided Him, saying, "He saved others; let Him save Himself, if He be the Christ, the chosen of God." ' Golgotha offered an ideal setting for such a crucifixion, and accommodation for all to behold 'The King of the Jews.' They could watch the soldiers mocking Him, and then playing dice for His garments at the foot of the Cross which bore the superscription in Greek, and Latin, and Hebrew 'This is the King of the Jews'.

We conducted a short service in the inspiring atmosphere of the garden, at a point where there were seats, supplied and maintained by American Christians. We meditated upon the events of Calvary and then descended the steps which led to the foot of Calvary's Hill to take a closer look at something else that had caught our eyes when we were assimilating the scene.

At the foot of the hill we noticed a doorway in the rock. There was no need to ask what it might be, because at the foot of the door, was a runnel, and we knew it was a sepulchre. The function of the runnel was to enable the circular stone to be rolled to the side when anyone wished to enter the sepulchre, and to replace it when it was to be closed off. This tomb was conveniently sited near to the scene of the crucifixion, and belonged to one Joseph of Arimathea (called by St Luke a counsellor, a good man, and a just one.) It was natural that with his deep sympathy for the Master, he should count it a privilege to offer his tomb for the burial of Jesus.

We went down to the sepulchre and looked in, thinking of that Easter morning when some of the disciples did the same thing. It was a small cell-like room with stone walls and contained nothing but a stone bench on the right hand side. Everything about it was simple and natural. St John records that the sepulchre 'was hewn in stone, wherein never before was man laid'. It looked the same still, and the open door was symbolic of the power of the resurrection.

St John further relates that 'in the place where he was crucified there was a garden; and in the garden a new sepulchre.' These words were satisfying, as we surveyed the garden in which we stood. It reached from the foot of Calvary's hill and enveloped the sepulchre. This aspect recalled for me something I had read in a little brochure, given to each of us by our tourist agency, *The Visitor's Guide to the Holy Land*, by David Edwards. Referring to the Garden Tomb, the author states, 'It does not carry the authority of a long tradition but it does comply with many of the requirements of such a site. It also captures the imagination and evokes an immediate experience.' That was exactly what we found. I am not sure of the logic that would base unquestioning credence simply on the antiquity of a tradition. However, in this day and age, one does not wish to be unnecessarily divisive or dogmatic, so whether one finds oneself at the Holy Sepulchre or the Garden Tomb, the crucial thing is to sense the spiritual help and conviction that emanate from the site whence the message of the Cross and the power of the resurrection find lodging in our soul.

Apart from the physical features of the Garden Tomb and the hill called Golgotha, we bear in mind a significant historic find. In the year A.D. 135 the Roman Emperor Hadrian erected a temple to Venus over the Tomb of the Resurrection. It was a defiant act of desecration. In the summer of 1924, a Miss Hussey found a stone which has since been identified as one of the shrine stones of the goddess Venus. This has proved to be a significant discovery, and possibly it lends strength to the theory that the Garden Tomb may be authentic. This tomb is associated with the name of General Gordon, a keen archaeologist, who was convinced that this was the true site, and hence, it is sometimes referred to as Gordon's Calvary. This is where he meditated and prayed.

On the day we visited the Garden Tomb there was only one thing that seemed to be out of place. To the right, and at the bottom of the steep face of Golgotha, there was a space which acted as a station for buses, and somehow they spoiled to some extent the atmosphere. One hopes that, by this time, this intrusion has been either removed or camouflaged.

Casting one more glance round the garden, and focussing my attention on the sepulchre for the last time, since the holiday was drawing to a close, I thought of that tender scene of Mary in the garden, standing perplexed, wondering what had happened. The stone had been rolled away, the tomb was empty, and it looked as if desecration had taken place. Whether it was in this garden or in the one associated with the Church of the Holy Sepulchre does not alter the experience. Mary, in her bewilderment, wept bitterly, and when asked by God's messengers, the angels 'Why are you weeping?' she answered, 'They have taken away my Lord, and I know not where they have laid Him.' While saying these words, she sensed the presence of someone standing behind her. It was Jesus, but, not expecting to see Him, she did not recognise Him through her tears. She assumed that He was the gardener and when He asked her the same question she said, 'If it is you, sir, who removed him, tell me where you have laid him, and I will take him away.' Jesus spoke her name — 'Mary'. She turned to Him and said 'Master.' What a wealth of communication took place in so few words — 'Mary' and 'Master'. The new age had begun. Life and immortality had come to light. The frightened and scattered disciples were reunited and spiritually revived in the power of the resurrection, as Jesus appeared to each group and individual according to the need.

The world could now live in the spirit of the Master to the end of the ages. The change that took place in the disciples was dramatic. Their fears and hesitations were conquered, and with growing experience and conviction, they preached in the name of the Lord.

Added to the power of the resurrection came the Ascension and the indwelling of the Holy Spirit. So the Spirit of the Lord reaches out to all the world. On a prominent point of the Mount of Olives stands a small octagonal Church with an open space in the roof, to symbolise the spot from which the Ascension took place. The house of John Mark is mentioned in the twentieth chapter of the Book of Acts as one of the venues where the early Church members met for prayer and fellowship. The Spirit was present there, as He is to be found where the twos and threes still meet in the Master's name.

By the time we had visited all these places we had come to the end of one of the greatest holidays we could ever have — a holiday that was enriched because it enshrined the root meaning of the word holiday, in that it was associated with holy days and holy things in the Holy Land. We had just enough time to visit some of the important buildings in the new sector of Jerusalem, including the Knesset which is Israel's House of Parliament. It is an artistic modern building, situated on a prominent hillside. Our guide informed us that the imposing, fifteen foot, symbolic seven-branched Candlestick was a gift from Britain to Israel. We also visited the Shrine of the Book, which is an attractive circular white building near to the new university. It stands impressively on the top of a hill. In shape it is like the lid of a jar — the architectural idea being inspired by the precious find of the Dead Sea Scrolls in a jar at Qumran. The scrolls consist of a copy of the writings of the prophet Isaiah, and they are on display in a twenty three foot long bronze case.

There is, of course, a limit to the ground one may cover on tour, but a holiday in Israel is so absorbing that it is remarkable what one can experience in a very short time. We were reluctant to pack our bags and get into the bus at our hotel when the time arrived for our departure. Down the hill we sped to Tel Aviv. After a most exhaustive searching of our baggage by airport officials, we boarded the plane. By the time we reached London via Zurich, and had changed to the flight for Belfast, we were beginning to feel a bit flat. Finally, we gathered with many others to collect our cases from the revolving luggage wheel. The party then dispersed in all directions as we made for our respective homes. We had parted with meagre salutations for we were all tired. It took a little time to retrieve our normal energy, and by then Israel seemed so far away — like a dream, but not a dream that fades. It had been for us the holiday of a lifetime.

If you were to ask what lasting impressions were created by our visit to the Holy Land, it would be possible to talk about all the things that gave us pleasure, but on the more reflective side, the outstanding feature is the feeling of how truly human Jesus was. We had a deep sense of the Son of Man. We could visualise Jesus in His background, wrestling with the problems of His day which have been so similar for each succeeding age. Every time we read of Jacob's Well, or Bethany, Bethlehem, Nazareth or Jerusalem, we keep looking at Him in His setting and keep hearing His words. Jesus becomes so human and so impressive in His humanity.

On the other hand we sense that we have come close to not only the Son of Man but also the Son of God, for as His divinity shines through His humanity, we realise more deeply and fundamentally how human God is, and yet how Divine.